# The
# Sun Will Rise Again

The Journey from Vanquished to Victorious

## Kristine Ohkubo

# DEDICATION

Although the figures vary between sources, World War II was without question the deadliest war in history. Of the estimated 70 million people killed, 50 to 55 million were civilians.

I would like to dedicate this book to the countless victims of war. The soldiers, the mothers, the fathers, the brothers, the sisters, the children, the dead, the living, and all those who suffered from the irrefutable aggression unleashed upon them.

May we learn from the past and never again demonstrate such hostility toward our fellow man.

# ACKNOWLEDGMENTS

I would like to express my gratitude to the many people who encouraged and supported me during this project. To all those who provided support, read, wrote, offered comments, shared their memories, and assisted in the editing, proofreading, and design of this book, thank you.

"The enemy is fear. We think it is hate; but it is fear."

-Gandhi

Japanese Empire in late 1941 - early 1942. The beginning of the Pacific War.

# TABLE OF CONTENTS

# INTRODUCTION

Although President Franklin D. Roosevelt signed the Neutrality Act on August 31, 1935, further cementing the United States' intention to stay out of foreign wars, he did explicitly state, "history is filled with unforeseeable situations that call for some flexibility of action." In other words, if the United States wished to join any given conflict, it could do so under the pretense of exercising the right to protect its citizens.

While the rest of the world had been embroiled in some type of battle since 1939, the United States continued to maintain its neutrality while indirectly contributing to the Allies' war effort.

"Indirect contribution" meant freely selling arms to countries which the United States deemed as friendly. When the Lend-Lease Act was signed into law on March 11, 1941, it enabled the U.S. to step up its military exports to the British in an effort to aid them in repelling Hitler's advancement toward England.

However, six years after the signing of the Neutrality Act, the unforeseeable situation which Roosevelt had eluded to came to pass, thus altering the United States' stance on the war. Instigated by the Empire of Japan, the attack on Pearl Harbor on December 7, 1941, came to be known as "a date which will live in infamy."

On December 8, President Roosevelt delivered a 10-minute speech in which he proclaimed, "The United States of America was suddenly and deliberately attacked by naval and air forces of the Empire of Japan. No matter how long it may take us to overcome this premeditated invasion, the American people in their righteous might will win through to absolute victory." The declaration of war on Japan was signed at 4:10 p.m. and the

United States officially entered the war, which it had to fight on two fronts: in Europe and the Pacific.

What prompted the Empire of Japan to attack the Pacific Fleet at Pearl Harbor? Was the attack really a surprise, or was it a carefully orchestrated event by Washington to anger the American public enough to want to go to war? What events unfolded leading up to Emperor Hirohito's radio address on August 15, 1945, during which he announced the surrender of Japan to the Allies?

This book focuses on the Pacific War. It will lead you through the Empire of Japan's provocation of the United States which led the United States to enter World War II, describe the gruesome events which unfolded on Japanese soil, provide you with comprehensive details of the hardships faced by Japanese Americans on American soil, and take you through the last stages of the war, which ultimately ended with the surrender of Japan. You will learn about the Japanese mindset during and after the war, what life was like during the seven-year American military occupation of Japan, and what Japan and her people had to face as they struggled to rebuild.

When World War II concluded, Japan was battered and the morale of its people was at an all-time low. However, in the land of the rising sun, the sun will rise again.

# KEY DATES DURING THE PACIFIC WAR

| 1941 | |
|---|---|
| December 7 | The Japanese attack Pearl Harbor and Wake Island. |
| December 8 | The Japanese attack Thailand, Guam, Malaya, Philippines, the Dutch East Indies and Hong Kong. |
| December 13 | The Japanese are victorious in Malaya (The Battle of Jitra). |
| December 23 | The Japanese are victorious in the Battle of Wake Island. |
| December 25 | The Japanese are victorious in the Battle of Hong Kong. |
| **1942** | |
| January 20 | The Japanese attack Burma. |
| January 23 | The Japanese attack New Guinea. |
| February 14 | The Japanese attack Sumatra. |
| February 15 | The Japanese are victorious in the Battle of Singapore. |
| February 18 | The Japanese attack Bali (The Battle of Badung Strait). |
| April 5-9 | The Japanese naval battle in the Indian Ocean (Battle of Ceylon/ Easter Sunday Raid). |
| April 18 | The Doolittle Raid–Air raid of Tokyo by the United States. |
| June 7 | The Japanese Navy is defeated at the Battle of Midway. |
| **1943** | |
| February 9 | The Japanese withdraw from Guadalcanal. |
| April 18 | Japanese Admiral Isoroku Yamamoto passes away. |

## 1944

| | |
|---|---|
| June 15 | The American forces land in Saipan. |
| July 5-13 | The Japanese retreat in Burma. |
| October 29 | The first Japanese kamikaze raid on the USS Intrepid. |
| November 17 | The first B-29 bomber raid of Tokyo. |

## 1945

| | |
|---|---|
| February 19 | The first amphibious assault of Iwo Jima by the American forces. |
| March 9-10 | The first Allied firebombing of Tokyo. |
| April 1 | The Allies invade Okinawa. |
| April 7 | The Japanese battleship Yamato is sunk. |
| April 12 | US President Franklin D. Roosevelt passes away. |
| August 6 | The United States drops an atomic bomb over Hiroshima. |
| August 9 | The United States drops an atomic bomb over Nagasaki. |
| August 15 | Japanese Emperor Hirohito announces the surrender of Japan. |
| September 2 | Japanese foreign affairs minister Mamoru Shigemitsu signs the Japanese Instrument of Surrender on board the USS Missouri. |

# THE PACIFIC WAR :
## *TAIHEIYO SENSO*

The war between Japan and China (the Second Sino-Japanese War) had been in progress since July 7, 1937, when Japan invaded Thailand, Malaya, Hong Kong, the Philippines and the Dutch East Indies (present day Indonesia) and attacked the military bases in Hawaii, Wake Island and Guam on December 7-8, 1941, effectively launching the Pacific War.

Although some may consider the Second Sino-Japanese War to be a part of World War II, the consensus is that World War II started in 1939 when England and France declared war on Nazi Germany following the invasion of Poland.

The Second Sino-Japanese War was a conflict fought primarily between the Empire of Japan and the Republic of China, with China receiving economic assistance from Germany, the Soviet Union and the United States. The war was the result of Japan's desire to secure access to raw material reserves and other economic resources such as food and labor. Japan's expansion into Asia was the result of the Japanese government's emulation of the West and Russia. Japanese imperialism came into play during a period of active expansion in China, and especially Russia's takeover of vast areas of Chinese territories during the nineteenth century. European expansion in the East was fueled by national pride, and the need for security, resources for industrialization, settlements for overpopulation, and ready markets for various manufactured goods. The Japanese embraced these goals too, but Japanese imperialism differed from Western imperialism as it arose only after facing colonization by the West.

Prior to Commodore Matthew Perry's visit to Japan on July 8, 1853, during which time he demanded a treaty permitting trade and the opening of Japanese ports to US merchant ships, Japan was in a period of national isolation.

This period, known as *Sakoku,* was characterized by a series of proclamations enacted by the Tokugawa shogunate under Tokugawa Iemitsu in 1633, which placed severe restrictions on the ability of foreigners to enter Japan. Japanese people were also forbidden to leave the country without special permission, on penalty of death if they returned. Although the closed country policy officially remained in effect until 1866, Perry's efforts to open Japan to Western trade eroded its enforcement significantly.

By all accounts, the Second Sino-Japanese War was the largest Asian war fought during the twentieth century resulting in an estimated 10-25 million Chinese civilian casualties and more than 4 million Chinese and Japanese military casualties.

However, the casualties in China were not simply limited to the conflict of war. There was a more sinister side to the Second Sino-Japanese War, which resulted in the deaths of at least 3,000 men, women and children. They were the victims of Unit 731.

Unit 731 was a covert biological and chemical warfare research and development unit of the Imperial Japanese Army that undertook lethal human experimentation during the Second Sino-Japanese War. Officially known as the Epidemic Prevention and Water Purification Department, it was headed by Surgeon General Shiro Ishii, a Japanese army medical officer and microbiologist. One of Ishii's main supporters was Colonel Chikahiko Koizumi, a Japanese military physician who became the Army Surgeon General of the Imperial Japanese Army in 1934. Koizumi and other Japanese army officers were interested in Germany's successful use of chlorine gas during the Second Battle of Ypres, Belgium (April 22–May 25, 1915) which killed 15,000 Allies, and thus wanted Japan to conduct their own research in the area of biological and chemical warfare. Koizumi served as Japan's Health Minister from 1941 to 1944.

Unit 731 originally set up shop in the Zhongma Fortress, located in Beiyinhe, Manchuria, a village 100 km (62 miles) south of Harbin. Following an explosion at the facility in 1935, Unit 731 was relocated to a much larger facility in Pingfang, approximately 24 km (15 miles) south of Harbin.

The experimental subjects were primarily supplied by the *Kempeitai* military police. The Kempeitai was equivalent to the Gestapo in Germany and known for both its brutality and the indiscriminate arrests of people with little or no evidence. Those who were arrested by the Kempeitai were presumed guilty and had little chance of receiving civilian help—and no chance to appeal for clemency. The Kempeitai officer was police investigator, prosecutor, judge, jury and executioner.

Although most of the victims Unit 731 experimented on were Chinese, a small percentage were Soviet, Mongolian, Korean and Allied POWs. The research was generously funded by the Japanese government until the war ended in 1945.

The Japanese researchers performed tests involving the bubonic plague, cholera, smallpox, botulism and other diseases. The research contributed to the development of the defoliation bacilli bomb and the flea bomb used to spread the bubonic plague. Other experiments included the effects of frostbite, venereal disease, and weapons such as grenades and flamethrowers.

In 1943, during the Battle of Changde, the Japanese army launched biological attacks infecting agriculture, reservoirs, wells, and other areas with anthrax, plague-carrying fleas, typhoid, dysentery, cholera, and other deadly pathogens. It is estimated that this attack killed at least 200,000 people. In addition to Chinese casualties, at least 1,700 Japanese in Chekiang were killed by their own country's biological weapons.

When the Russians invaded Manchuria in 1945, the 731 facilities were abandoned in haste. The majority of the Unit 731 members and their families fled to Japan. Ishii ordered every member of the group to take the secret to their graves, threatening to find them if they failed. The remaining crew were issued potassium cyanide vials in the event they were captured.

The skeleton crew left behind was responsible for blowing up the facility and killing the remaining prisoners. Their bodies were incinerated in an effort to destroy all evidence.

During the occupation of Japan, General MacArthur granted immunity to the physicians of Unit 731, including Ishii, in exchange for providing the United States with information pertaining to research on biological warfare and data from human experimentation. The occupation authorities monitored the activities of former unit members, including reading and censoring their mail. This information was not shared with other members of the Allied group.

The Soviet Union conducted their own military trials in December of 1949. During this time they prosecuted twelve top military leaders and scientists from Unit 731. They received sentences ranging from two to twenty-five years in a Siberian labor camp. The trial transcripts were published in various languages, including English. The United States refused to acknowledge these trials, branding them to be nothing more than communist propaganda.

The Soviet Union constructed a biological weapons facility in Sverdlovsk after World War II using documentation captured from Unit 731 in Manchuria.

After Japan attacked Pearl Harbor, the Second Sino-Japanese War was merged into the greater conflict of World War II in what became known as the Pacific War.

On December 10, 1941, the Japanese cabinet selected the name *Dai Toa Senso* (Greater East Asia War) to refer to both the war with the Western Allies and the ongoing war with China. However, during the American military occupation of Japan from 1945 to 1952, this Japanese term was prohibited from being used in official documents. Instead, the term *Taiheiyo Senso* (Pacific War) was adopted to describe the aforementioned conflicts.

With imported oil comprising over 80% of domestic consumption, Japan was in perpetual need of fresh resources. Consequently, in 1935 the Japanese military strategists targeted the Dutch East Indies for its rich oil reserves. By 1940, the target area had grown to include Indo-China (Southeast Asia), Malaya, and the Philippines. As Japan built up its military presence in key strategic locations, Australia, the United States, and Great Britain imposed embargos on Japan cutting off oil, iron ore and steel imports. Since these were the raw materials Japan desperately needed to continue its conquests, the Japanese government regarded the embargos as acts of aggression that would lead to Japan's economic collapse. As a result, in April of 1941, the *Daihonei* (the Japanese Imperial General Headquarters) began preparations for war with the Western powers.

The Daihonei intended to launch a limited war in which Japan would seize key objectives and establish a defensive perimeter against counterattacks by the Pacific Fleet stationed at Pearl Harbor. The Japanese leaders were well aware that total military victory against the United States was impossible, and they hoped to negotiate for peace after securing their initial victories.

The attack on Pearl Harbor was launched during the early morning hours of December 7, 1941. The Japanese air strike damaged eight battleships, destroyed 188 aircraft, and killed 2,403 Americans.

However, the Japanese plan to force the United States into a negotiated settlement failed, as the American losses were less serious than initially anticipated. Of the eight battleships stationed at Pearl Harbor, four were damaged and only four were sunk. All but the USS Arizona were later raised and six were returned to service. Additionally, the more formidable American aircraft carriers were out at sea during the attack, and the vital naval infrastructure consisting of fuel oil tanks, shipyard facilities, and a power station were left untouched.

Directly after the assault, questions were raised as to how and why the United States had been caught so off guard. In the years that followed, accusations emerged that American government officials had advance knowledge of Japan's attack on Pearl Harbor.

The United States had lost over 100,000 soldiers during World War I and the American public were vehemently opposed to entering another European war. President Roosevelt knew that if he approached Congress and asked for a declaration of war against Germany, Congress certainly would not have consented to it. The only way in which Congress would declare war against Germany would be if Germany attacked the United States first.

President Roosevelt tried in vain to induce Germany to attack the United States but Germany refused to take the bait. The President's attempts included everything from having US warships escort British ships in war zones to tracking and reporting the location of German submarines in the area. Germany was well aware that US intervention in World War I had brought about Germany's defeat; therefore, they had no intention of engaging the United States in World War II.

This led Roosevelt to shift his focus to Japan. If Japan were to attack the United States, it would afford a back door opportunity for the United States to enter the war.

With their assets frozen in the United States, and with the embargos choking off the necessary materials which Japan desperately needed, the Japanese government was left with no choice but to attack the Pacific Fleet.

Immediately following the attack on Pearl Harbor, President Roosevelt appointed a commission chaired by Supreme Court Justice Owen Roberts (the Roberts Commission) to investigate and report the facts relating to the attack. The commission presented their findings to Congress on January 28, 1942, citing Admiral Husband Kimmel and General Walter Short, the field commanders in Hawaii, for dereliction of duty. Since the Roberts Commission was not a trial, the commanders were denied all the traditional rights provided to defendants in a court case. As a result, and with the aid of the press, Kimmel and Short were portrayed as traitors and inundated with hate mail and death threats.

The public demanded that Admiral Kimmel and General Short be tried by court-martial, but the Roosevelt administration initially resisted due to the fear that the government's secrets would be revealed during the court proceedings. The administration contemplated the idea of retiring Kimmel and Short, but ultimately decided to move forward with the court-martials. A three-year statute of limitations applied to the charges, and the administration knew that if they delayed the court-martials long enough the officers could not be charged. Playing on the public's fears about safety during the war, the administration announced that the court-martials would be postponed "until such time as the public interest and safety would permit." By taking this course of action, the administration successfully satisfied the public's outrage — for the time being.

Admiral Kimmel and General Short, however, saw court-martials as the only means of clearing themselves, and they both voluntarily waived the statute of limitations.

The court-martials moved forward. The Naval Court of Inquiry, spearheaded by Admiral Orin Murfin, convened from July 24 to September 27, 1944. The Court concluded that Admiral Harold Stark, the Chief of Naval Operations, did not apprise Admiral Kimmel of all of the information which Washington possessed. The Court determined that having this information would have enabled Admiral Kimmel to have a more complete picture of the situation and be better prepared to defend against the attack. The conclusion reached by the Roberts Commission was dismissed. Admiral Kimmel was exonerated of all charges.

Similarly, the Army Pearl Harbor Board chaired by Lieutenant General George Grunert met from July 20 to October 20, 1944. The Board found that General George Marshall and the War Department failed to keep General Short fully informed of the deteriorating state of US–Japanese affairs. It further stated that Short did not receive critical information on the evening of December 6 and on the morning of December 7. The Board also cited General Leonard Gerow, the Chief of the Army's War Plans Division for failing to keep the Hawaiian field commander informed of the Japanese moves that were known in Washington.

The failure to disseminate critical information to the field commanders was further reinforced by bringing to light the scores of Magic intercepts that were kept from Admiral Kimmel and

General Short.

Magic was an Allied cryptanalysis project utilized during World War II. It involved the US Army's Signals Intelligence Service (SIS) and the Naval Communications Code and Signal Unit.

Since the 1920s, the Japanese Navy had relied on code books to send encrypted messages. Although the code books were changed regularly, the code was generally weak and easily broken.

In 1923, an incident involving breaking and entering into the Japanese consulate in New York yielded photographs of the code book's pages. These photographs aided cryptologists to some degree but the actual breaking of the code was greatly delayed by the lack of intercepted telegrams. The Japanese Navy was not engaged in significant battle operations before Pearl Harbor; therefore, there was little traffic available to provide the raw material necessary for the codebreakers to work with.

Finally, in 1926, Agnes Driscoll and Lieutenant Joseph Rochefort managed to break the Japanese code referred to as the RED CODE. Agnes Driscoll was a mathematics, physics, foreign languages and music major. She was recruited as a Navy Chief Yeoman in 1918 and worked at the Naval Communications Code and Signal Unit. The processed code messages were kept in classified top secret red-colored folders, hence the term RED.

The Japanese became suspicious that their code had been broken and abandoned the RED CODE in November of 1930, replacing it with a more complex code system referred to as the BLUE CODE. Once again, the naming of the code was arbitrary and based on the two blue-covered loose leaf binders in which the messages were stored. In September of 1931, Agnes Driscoll was able to sufficiently decipher the new code, which the Japanese Navy continued to use until 1939.

In 1939, the Japanese Navy began using the Navy General Operational Code (referred to as JN25 by the US). JN25 was a code that produced five-numeral groups for transmission. It became the most popular and secure communication system used by the Japanese naval forces. It wasn't until late May 1942 when the code was finally broken and the intercepted messages provided the critical forewarning of the Japanese attack on Midway.

During the autumn of 1939, with Germany's assistance, Japan also began to employ modified Enigma machines to send coded messages. Enigma machines were a series of electro-mechanical rotor cipher machines invented by German engineer Arthur Scherbius at the end of World War I.

The first Enigma machine was obtained from the Germans by Japanese Baron Hiroshi Oshima. As a colonel, Oshima was dispatched to Berlin as a military attaché in 1934. He was promoted to Major General in March of 1935 and met with Adolph Hitler privately that fall.

In 1937, the Japanese succeeded in building a modified Enigma machine which they called *97-shiki injiki* (type 97 typewriter). Its chief designer was Kazuo Tanabe. The machine consisted of two typewriters and an electrical rotor system with a 25-character alphabetic switchboard. Unlike the Enigma machine, which transmitted the messages in the form of blinking lights, the 97-shiki injiki would transmit the encrypted messages to the second typewriter, which then produced the transmission on a piece of paper. This was a huge advancement from the German Enigma machine, which required two people to operate it—one to type the message and another to record the projections. The 97-shiki injiki only required one person and reduced the likelihood of human error. However, the system was too bulky and cumbersome to be used out in the field and was reserved for diplomatic communications only.

The new code employed by the Japanese utilizing the 97-shiki injiki proved to be a challenge because the key changed daily, yielding over 70,000,000,000,000 possible arrangements which would determine the method of encryption.

In 1939, the United States Army hired cryptography expert William Friedman to help break the new code. Eighteen months into his work, Friedman suffered a mental breakdown and was institutionalized. Fortunately, he had completed sufficient work enabling eight functional replicas of the machine to be created by the United States. Unfortunately, having the replica machines did not mean that the messages could be broken because the daily keys being used were still unknown to code breakers. In time, Lieutenant Francis Raven discovered a pattern being employed by the Japanese in their daily keys. With this new discovery, the final pieces of the puzzle fell into place and the code was broken. The new code was codenamed PURPLE (a combination of the previous code names, RED and BLUE). The information gained from decryptions of the 97-shiki injiki was eventually code-named Magic.

When the Naval Court of Inquiry convened, a source inside the United States Department of the Navy had tipped Admiral Kimmel and his attorneys about the numerous Magic intercepts kept from the Admiral in 1941. Although they were difficult to obtain, the intercepts, 43 in all, were eventually delivered to the Court.

The Army Pearl Harbor Board, after receiving news of the Magic intercepts, were also able to secure copies from the War Department files. Upon the conclusion of the hearings, the Board issued its report, which included the following statement. "Up to the morning of December 7, 1941, everything that the Japanese were planning to do was known to the United States except the very hour and minute when bombs were falling on Pearl Harbor."

Distressed by the court findings, the administration and the Pentagon announced that, in the interest of national security, the court-martial results would not become public until the war's end. The press was informed that the Naval Court of Inquiry had marked its conclusions top secret, and therefore nothing could be published.

Shocked by the announcement, Admiral Murfin, who had spearheaded the Naval Court of Inquiry protested, pointing out that while the breaking of the Japanese diplomatic code was not meant for public knowledge, the Court had only marked part of its determinations top secret. Nevertheless, the reports issued by the Court were suppressed.

The suppression of the reports enabled Washington to buy more time to conduct its own inquiries into the matter, which it claimed would supplement the court-martials.

Lieutenant Colonel Henry Clausen was chosen to head the War Department's investigations. Admiral Kent Hewitt, and John Sonnett, a special assistant to the Navy Secretary, were appointed to participate in the investigations by Navy Secretary, James Forrestal.

In a blow to Admiral Kimmel and General Short, the witnesses who had testified against Washington during the court-martials reversed their testimonies when they were questioned by the War Department. Colonel Rufus S. Bratton was one of those witnesses. During his testimony to the Army Pearl Harbor Board, he stated that he had delivered the first 13 parts of a 14 part message pertaining to Japan breaking off negotiations with the United States to General Marshall and General Gerow via his secretary. When questioned by the War Department, he denied that the deliveries were ever made. Incidentally, part 14 of the message called for the destruction of code books and indicated that hostilities of some sort would begin at 1 p.m., Eastern Standard Time.

Other officers also retracted their original statements. The court-martial proceedings had gathered testimony from these officers about a message from Tokyo to its Washington embassy delivered on November 19, which they now denied seeing. This message came to be known as the winds instruction and read as follows:

*In case of emergency (danger of cutting off our diplomatic relations), and the cutting off of international communications, the following warning will be added in the middle of the daily Japanese language short wave news broadcast:*

*(1) In case of Japan–US relations endangered: Higashi no kaze ame (East wind, rain)*
*(2) Japan–USSR relations endangered: Kita no kaze kumori (North wind, cloudy)*
*(3) Japan–British relations endangered: Nishi no kaze hare (West wind, clear)*

What was the reason for this sudden change of heart? It could be presumed that all of the witnesses were career military men. If they upheld their testimony, they would possibly risk jeopardizing their future careers.

Despite the various retractions, there was one man who stood by his testimony and refused to bend. That man was Captain Laurance Safford.

Captain Safford had testified before the Naval Court of Inquiry that he had seen the winds message. He later wrote about his meeting with John Sonnett, stating that "His purpose seemed to be to refute testimony that was unfavorable to anyone in Washington."

There appeared to be a huge cover-up in progress. It wasn't surprising to Captain Safford, for he had discovered that all copies of the winds message along with other important Pearl Harbor memos contained in the Navy files had been destroyed.

Four days following the attack on Pearl Harbor, Rear Admiral Leigh Noyes issued a directive to "Destroy all notes or anything in writing." The order was illegal, as naval memos can only be destroyed through a directive issued by Congress, but that did not prevent the orders from being carried out. Meanwhile, rumors circulated that the War Department had also purged its files.

With the Clausen and Hewitt inquiries over, the Army and the Navy issued a joint announcement on August 29, 1945.

Blame was once again shifted to General Short and Admiral Kimmel. As a result, the American public never really knew what the court-martials had determined.

Ultimately, there were eight hearings held over the course of World War II, culminating in a joint congressional investigation beginning on November 15, 1945. In 1946, the congressional committee's findings were released, in which a majority of the blame was assigned to the Hawaiian field commanders. The committee also blamed the manner in which the War and Navy departments handled the matter, but they were careful to leave President Roosevelt's reputation untarnished.

General Short passed away in 1949 and Admiral Kimmel in 1968. Their ranks were never restored despite the Congressional probe conducted in 1995 at the urging of the families of both men.

However, on May 25, 1999, the United States Senate passed a resolution that cleared Kimmel and Short of dereliction of duty. Senator William Roth of Delaware said, "They were denied vital intelligence that was available in Washington," with Senator Strom Thurmond from South Carolina adding that Kimmel and Short were "the two final victims of Pearl Harbor."

Scapegoating the Hawaiian field commanders for the attack on Pearl Harbor was not enough, however. In retaliation for Japan's attack, President Roosevelt enacted Executive Order 9066, which called for the relocation and incarceration of Japanese Americans.

Although the US condemned the Nazi regime for operating concentration camps in Europe between 1933 and 1945, that condemnation did not prevent the US government from establishing a series of Detention Camps, Temporary Detention Centers and Department of Justice Camps throughout the United States, used primarily for citizens of Japanese ancestry residing in the United States and Latin America.

The first Nazi concentration camp, Dachau, was set up in 1933. The concentration camp was not the same as the extermination camp. The extermination camps were constructed with the specific purpose of mass murdering Jews and other ethnic groups deemed undesirable by the Nazi regime. Initially, the first inmates in concentration camps consisted of Hitler's political opponents. Later, the camp population grew to include Jews, gypsies and criminals. Although the purpose of concentration camps differed from extermination camps, imprisonment in a concentration camp meant inhuman forced labor, brutal mistreatment, hunger, disease and random executions. Several hundred thousand people died in the concentration camps.

During 1942, the Allies obtained reports of a Nazi plan to murder all the Jews. These reports included details on methods, numbers and locations. On December 17, 1942, the Allies issued a proclamation condemning the extermination of the Jewish people in Europe and declared that they would punish the perpetrators.

Although the US did not exterminate Japanese Americans, the government established detention camps and subjected the detainees to extremely harsh conditions nonetheless. There were ten permanent detention camps that were home to relocated Japanese Americans from 1942 to 1946. These included:

1. Amache (Granada), Colorado - In operation from August 24, 1942 until October 15, 1945. (Highest population recorded 7,318 people.)
2. Gila River, Arizona – In operation from July 20, 1942 until November 10, 1945. (Highest population recorded 13,348 people.)
3. Heart Mountain, Wyoming – In operation from August 12, 1942 until November 10, 1945. (Highest population recorded 10,767 people.)
4. Jerome, Arkansas – In operation from October 6, 1942 until June 30, 1944. (Highest population recorded 8,497 people.)

5. Manzanar, California – In operation from June 1, 1942 until November 21, 1945. (Highest population recorded 10,046 people.)
6. Minidoka, Idaho – In operation from August 10, 1942 until October 28, 1945. (Highest population recorded 9,397 people.)
7. Poston (Colorado River), Arizona – In operation from May 8, 1942 until November 28, 1945. (Highest population recorded 17,814 people.)
8. Rohwer, Arkansas – In operation from September 18, 1942 until November 30, 1945. (Highest population recorded 8,475 people.)
9. Topaz (Central Utah), Utah – In operation from September 11, 1942 until October 31, 1945. (Highest population recorded 8,130 people.)
10. Tule Lake, California – In operation from May 27, 1942 until March 20, 1946. (Highest population recorded 18,789 people.)

In addition to the permanent detention camps, the government also established 16 temporary detention centers that were used from late March 1942 until mid-October 1942. These camps were used to house the relocated Japanese Americans until they could be moved into the ten permanent internment centers.

The temporary sites were located in highly visible and public locations. It would have been impossible for the local populace to say that they were unaware of the removal and imprisonment of Japanese Americans.

The temporary detention camps were located as follows:

1. Fresno, California

2. Manzanar, California (from March 21, 1942 until June 1, 1942, when it was converted into a permanent camp).
3. Marysville, California
4. Mayer, Arizona
5. Merced, California
6. Pinedale, California
7. Portland, Oregon
8. Puyallup, Washington
9. Sacramento, California
10. Salinas, California
11. Santa Anita, California
12. Tanforan, San Bruno, California
13. Tulare, California
14. Turlock, Byron, California

Finally, the United States government utilized 27 Department of Justice Camps to house 2,260 individuals of Japanese descent that they classified as "dangerous persons." These people were taken from 12 Latin American countries, with the largest group (1,800 individuals) coming from Peru.

The American government wanted to use these individuals to bargain for potential hostage exchanges with Japan. At the conclusion of the war, 1,400 of these detainees were prevented from returning to their home country of Peru and 900 were actually deported to Japan. Of the remaining 500, 300 took their cases to court and were allowed to settle in Seabrook, New Jersey.

The Department of Justice Camps were located in:

1. Santa Fe, New Mexico
2. Bismark, North Dakota
3. Crystal City, Texas

4. Missoula, Montana
5. Seagoville, Texas
6. Kooskia, Idaho

There were 127,000 Japanese Americans living in the continental United States at the time of the attack on Pearl Harbor. Of that number, 112,000 lived on the West Coast. Approximately 80,000 were *nisei* (second generation, American-born Japanese with United States citizenship) and *sansei* (third generation, the children of the nisei). The remainder were *issei* (first generation immigrants born in Japan who were ineligible for United States citizenship by United States' law).

Although Executive Order 9066 did not specifically spell out that all persons of Japanese ancestry were to be forcibly relocated, it did authorize regional military commanders to designate certain military areas from which any or all persons could be excluded. This authorization was used to declare that all Japanese Americans were excluded from the entire West Coast, except for those already in government camps. By March of 1942, approximately 5,000 Japanese Americans voluntarily relocated outside of the exclusion zone. Another 5,500 community leaders had been arrested after the attack on Pearl Harbor and were already in custody. The remainder of the mainland Japanese Americans were forcibly relocated during the spring of 1942.

The US government also relocated orphaned children of Japanese descent, some of whom were only of one eighth of Japanese ancestry. These children were taken from three California orphanages: the Shonien or Japanese Children's Home of Los Angeles, the Maryknoll Home in Los Angeles and the Salvation Army Home in San Francisco, and relocated to the Manzanar Children's Village, an orphanage within Manzanar. A total of 101 orphans were housed in the Manzanar Children's Village from June of 1942 to September of 1945.

But not all Japanese Americans went quietly. Fred Toyosaburo Korematsu, Gordon Hirabayashi and Minoru Yasui were three challengers who took their cases all the way to the US Supreme Court. The Supreme Court also heard the case of Mitsuye Endo, a 22-year-old California woman selected by attorney James C. Purcell as a suitable plaintiff to challenge the incarceration of Japanese Americans through a habeas corpus petition.

Fred Toyosaburo Korematsu was born in Oakland, California in 1919. He challenged the relocation orders and became a fugitive. He was arrested and jailed. Later, with the aid of civil rights attorney Wayne M. Collins, his case against the United States was brought to the Supreme Court.

Wayne M. Collins, born in Sacramento, California, worked on cases related to the Japanese American evacuation and internment. He was one of the founders of the ACLU of Northern California and served as its director.

It is important to note that in August of 1945, Collins began advising Japanese American internees deceived or coerced into renouncing their American citizenship under the Renunciation Act of 1944 of their legal rights.

Enacted by the 78th Congress, the Renunciation Act of 1944 enabled people physically present in the US to renounce their citizenship when the country was in a state of war by making an application to the Attorney General. Prior to the law's passage, it was not possible to lose United States citizenship while on United States' territory except by conviction for treason. The intention of the 1944 Act was to encourage Japanese American internees to renounce their citizenship so that they could be deported to Japan.

Collins also represented over 2,000 Japanese Latin Americans detained by the US in the Department of Justice Camps, whom the government intended to barter for American prisoners of war. While most were deported after the war as "undesirable aliens," Collins successfully enabled hundreds to remain and make their homes in the United States.

Fred Korematsu was one of four sons born to his Japanese parents, Kotsui Aoki and Kakusaburo Korematsu, who immigrated to the United States in 1905. Fred's exposure to racism came when he was only a high school student. He encountered an army recruiting officer who told him, "We have orders not to accept you." The parents of his Italian girlfriend were also prejudiced toward him. They told him that people of Japanese descent were inferior and unfit to mix with white people.

He eventually managed to register with the Selective Service but he was rejected due to stomach ulcers. Determined to contribute his services to the defense effort, he trained instead to become a welder and found a position at a shipyard. Following the attack on Pearl Harbor, Fred's Japanese heritage caused him to lose his job at the shipyard. He found another job soon afterward but was fired a week later for the same reason.

After Executive Order 9066 was signed, Korematsu underwent plastic surgery on his eyelids in the hope of passing as a Caucasian. He changed his name to Clyde Sarahand and claimed to be of Spanish and Hawaiian heritage.

On May 3, 1942, Japanese Americans were ordered to assembly centers as a prelude to being removed to the internment camps. Korematsu refused to go and went into hiding in the Oakland area. He was arrested in San Leandro on May 30, 1942 and jailed in San Francisco. While in jail, he was approached by Ernest Besig, the director of the American Civil Liberties Union (ACLU) of Northern California and asked whether he would be willing to use his case to test the legality of Executive Order 9066. Korematsu agreed.

Many of the high ranking ACLU members were close to President Roosevelt, and they urged Besig not to take Korematsu's case. Besig ignored their pleas.

When Korematsu was arraigned on June 18, 1942, Besig posted $5,000 bail on his behalf and the two men attempted to leave the court. They were met by military police and Korematsu was taken into custody and confined at the Presidio, a US Army military fort in San Francisco.

On September 8, 1942, Korematsu was tried and convicted in federal court for violating Public Law No. 503. The law stated that violating military orders issued under the authority of Executive Order 9066 would be considered a criminal act. He was placed on five years' probation and taken to the Tanforan Assembly Center. Later, he and his family were transferred to the Central Utah War Relocation Center located in Topaz, Utah.

Korematsu appealed his case to the United States Court of Appeals. He was granted a review on March 27, 1943, but the original verdict was upheld. He appealed once again and brought his case to the United States Supreme Court, which granted a review on March 27, 1944. On December 18, 1944, in a 6–3 decision, the Court stated that compulsory exclusion, though constitutionally suspect, is justified during circumstances of "emergency and peril."

In 1983, the United States District Court in San Francisco formally vacated Korematsu's conviction. At the time, he told Judge

Marilyn Patel that instead of a legal pardon, he wanted to be assured that the US government would never again take such an action.

"If anyone should do any pardoning," he said, "I should be the one pardoning the government for what they did to the Japanese American people."

Gordon Hirabayashi was born in Sandpoint, Washington on April 23, 1918. Gordon's parents, Shungo and Mitsuko Hirabayashi, both came from a farming community in the Nagano prefecture in Japan. His father, Shungo, immigrated to the United States in 1907 along with seven of his classmates. Seven years later, in an arranged marriage, Shungo was matched with Mitsuko, who joined him in the United States in 1914. Both Shungo and Mitsuko had studied at the Kenshi Gijuku academy in Japan, where they learned English and converted to Christianity before coming to the United States.

After graduating from high school, Gordon Hirabayashi enrolled at the University of Washington. He also registered with the Selective Service as a conscientious objector.

When Executive Order 9066 was signed, Hirabayashi was confident that as a citizen, his rights would be protected. He quit school and volunteered with the American Friends Service Committee, an organization which aided families by arranging for the storage of their belongings prior to being incarcerated.

When travel restrictions and curfews were established against Japanese Americans, Hirabayashi ignored the rules and went about his business as a law-abiding citizen. When it came time to register for relocation, he turned himself in to the FBI with the intention of creating a case to test the government's right to incarcerate Japanese Americans without the due process of law.

He was represented by Arthur G. Barnett, a Bainbridge Island lawyer, and his case was funded by a defense fund organized by Mary Farquharson, a politician and lawyer for the University District of the ACLU.

When Hirabayashi was taken into custody, the FBI agents discovered his diary, containing entries in which he discussed his decision not to obey the curfew. Based on this evidence and his stated intention of refusing to obey the exclusion order, Hirabayashi was indicted on May 28, 1942 for violating Public Law No. 505, which made violating Civilian Exclusion Order No. 57 and curfew a federal crime.

When Hirabayashi's team of lawyers appealed his case to the Supreme Court, instead of ruling on the issue of the constitutionality of exclusion, the court only considered his conviction for disobeying curfew, and thus his conviction was upheld. He served his sentence at the Tucson Federal Prison.

Upon his release from Tucson Federal Prison, he received the "loyalty" questionnaire, or Selective Service Form 304A, which he refused to complete. Despite his refusal he was still ordered for induction. He did not appear as ordered and was charged with Selective Service violations. As a result, he was given a short one-year sentence at the McNeil Island Penitentiary.

After the war, Hirabayashi continued his education at the University of Washington, where he earned his B.A., M.A., and Ph.D. degrees in sociology. In 1959, he joined the faculty at the University of Alberta, where he served as the chair of sociology from 1970 to 1975.

After his retirement in 1983, he was asked by a team of lawyers if he wanted his case re-opened, to which he agreed. The Ninth Circuit Court of Appeals ruled in favor of Hirabayashi's case, vacating his personal conviction in 1987.

Hirabayashi passed away on January 2, 2012, at age 93. In May of 2012, he was posthumously awarded the Presidential Medal of Freedom by President Obama, the highest civilian honor to be awarded.

Minoru Yasui was born in Hood River, Oregon on October 19, 1916. He was the third son in a family of nine children. His parents, Shizuyo and Masuo Yasui were fruit farmers. At age eight he was sent to Japan, where he spent the summer. When he returned to Oregon, he was enrolled in a Japanese language school for three years. Yasui earned his bachelor's degree from the University of Oregon in 1937 and went on to earn his law degree from the University of Oregon Law School in 1939. Unable to find work as a Japanese American, he took a position at the Japanese Consulate General of Chicago as a speechwriter.

Following the attack on Pearl Harbor, Yasui quit his consular job and returned to Oregon. He had been a Reserve Officer Training Corps cadet while in college and was commissioned as a second lieutenant in the Army Reserves after he graduated. He was initially ordered to report to Fort Vancouver in Washington but when he arrived for duty, he was turned away due to his Japanese ancestry. He attempted to enlist nine times and was turned away each time.

Yasui opened a law practice dedicated to helping the Japanese community. He was the only attorney of Japanese heritage in Portland at the time.

On March 28, 1942, Yasui walked through the streets of downtown Portland after curfew and demanded to be arrested. The policeman he encountered brushed him off and told him to go home. Determined, he marched into the police station and demanded to be arrested. This time, the officer on duty obliged.

He was convicted of challenging the curfew law and lost his appeal in the Supreme Court. He spent nine months at the Multnomah County Jail in Portland before being sent to the Minidoka Relocation Camp in Idaho.

In the summer of 1944, Yasui was allowed to leave the internment camp and found work in Chicago. In September that same year, he moved to Denver, Colorado. He passed the bar exam in June of 1945, but was denied admission to the state's bar because of his wartime criminal record. He appealed to the Colorado Supreme Court and won his case.

Yasui continued to fight his wartime arrest record until his death on November 12, 1986. In 1983, he filed a motion requesting the court to reverse his conviction. He also requested the court to find that the proclamation under which he had been convicted for breaking curfew was unconstitutional. The district court vacated his conviction but did not find that the government had acted unconstitutionally. He appealed to the Ninth Circuit Court of Appeals who dismissed the case after his death. The Supreme Court agreed with the Appeals Court's decision and Yasui's case was finally closed.

In November of 2015, members of the Yasui family were invited to the White House, where President Barack Obama posthumously bestowed the Presidential Medal of Freedom upon him.

Mitsuye Endo was born on May 10, 1920 in Sacramento, California. She was the daughter of issei parents and the second of four children. After graduating from high school, she attended secretarial school and secured a clerical position with the State Department of Employment. Following the attack on Pearl

Harbor, she, along with 300-500 Japanese American state employees, lost her job. She and her family were sent to the Sacramento Assembly Center and later transferred to the Tule Lake internment camp.

Meanwhile, the Japanese American Citizens League hired attorney James C. Purcell to help challenge the incarceration of nisei. Purcell selected Mitsuye because she represented the ideal candidate. She had been raised a Methodist, did not speak or read Japanese, had never visited Japan and had a brother serving in the US Army.

Purcell sent a representative to speak with Mitsuye to determine if she would be willing to file a lawsuit. She was hesitant at first but eventually agreed to do it. A petition was filed on July 12, 1942 in the federal district court in San Francisco. The court offered to release her from the camp, provided she dropped her case and promised not to return to the West Coast. She refused, and her case made its way to the United States Supreme Court.

As her case went through the various courts, the army opened up the West Coast to loyal Japanese Americans. Mitsuye was segregated and moved to Topaz, Utah where she remained for the next two years.

On December 19, 1944, the Supreme Court ruled in favor of Mitsuye Endo but failed to address the fundamental question of constitutional rights. Mitsuye left Topaz in May of 1945 and settled in with her sister in Chicago. She eventually took a secretarial position with the Mayor's Committee on Race Relations and kept a low profile for the remainder of her life. She married Kenneth Tsutsumi, whom she had met in camp and they had three children together. Mitsuye Endo passed away on April 14, 2006 after losing her battle with cancer.

Interestingly, Japanese Americans were not the only ones incarcerated during World War II. When President Roosevelt signed Executive Order 9066, it paved the way for the roundup of Japanese Americans and it also led to the arrest of Germans and Italians, whom the FBI considered to be security risks and labeled as enemy aliens. There were 264 Italians and 1,296 Germans arrested by the FBI in 1941. By the end of the war, over 31,000 suspected enemy aliens and their families, including a few Jewish refugees from Nazi Germany, had been interned at Immigration and Naturalization Services (INS) internment camps and military facilities throughout the United States.

One Caucasian woman was interned at the Heart Mountain internment camp along with her Japanese American husband during this time. Her name was Estelle Peck Ishigo.

Estelle Peck Ishigo was born in Oakland, California on July 15, 1899. She was the daughter of a concert singer and a portrait and landscape artist. While attending the Otis Art Institute she met a San Franciscan nisei, Arthur Shigeharu Ishigo. The couple were married in Mexico in 1928 as inter-racial marriage did not become legal in California until 1948.

Following the attack on Pearl Harbor, she and her husband both lost their jobs. When her husband was ordered to report to the Pomona Assembly Center, Estelle opted to join him and the two were eventually incarcerated at Heart Mountain in Wyoming. During their incarceration at the camp, Estelle chronicled their daily lives through her drawings and paintings.

After their release from the internment camp, the couple lived in a trailer camp in Southern California. Arthur passed away in 1957. In 1972, Estelle published a book called *Lone Heart Mountain*, which related her experiences at the Heart Mountain camp and included her drawings. The same year, the California Historical Society exhibited her artwork in an exhibition called *Months of Waiting*.

Sadly, she was found by the former Heart Mountain detainees in 1983, living in poverty and having lost both of her legs to gangrene. She became the subject of Steven Okazaki's Academy Award winning film, *Days of Waiting*, just prior to her death in 1990. Estelle Peck Ishigo passed away in Los Angeles on February 25, 1990.

The United States was not alone in confining persons of Japanese heritage to internment camps; Canada also had internment camps.

Tension between Canadians and Japanese immigrants existed long before the outbreak of World War II. Negative beliefs and fears about Asian immigrants began to surface as early as 1858 with the influx of Asians into British Columbia during the Fraser Canyon Gold Rush.

When news of the Pearl Harbor attack reached Canada, years of smoldering fear and resentment against Japanese Canadians exploded into panic and anger in British Columbia. There were approximately 22,000 Japanese Canadians residing in Canada's westernmost province at the time; and although fears of sabotage and disloyalty were unfounded, the US's entry into war provided a convenient excuse for Canadians to act on their anti-Asian sentiments.

Within days after the Pearl Harbor attack, the Canadian Pacific Railway fired all of its Japanese employees, with other industries following suit. Japanese fisherman were ordered to stay in port and their boats were seized by the Canadian Navy.

During the Battle of Hong Kong (December 8–25, 1941), 2,000 Canadian soldiers were killed or imprisoned by the Japanese forces. This event intensified the persecution of Japanese Canadians.

Following the example set by the United States, British Colombia declared a 100-mile strip of land along the coast as an exclusion zone on January 14, 1942. All Japanese Canadian men between the ages of 18 and 45 were ordered out of the exclusion zone and sent to road camps.

On March 4, 1942, that order was expanded to include all people of Japanese descent. They were told to pack a single suitcase and were taken to holding areas, from which point they would be taken to areas inland. Some families waited in these holding areas for months before being relocated to the camps.

The internment camps and relocation centers were located as follows:

British Columbia

1. Bay Farm
2. Greenwood
3. Kaslo
4. Lemon Creek
5. New Denver
6. Popoff
7. Rosebery

8. Sandon
9. Slocan City
10. Bridge River (South Shalalth)
11. McGillivray Falls
12. Minto City
13. East Lillooet
14. Sunshine Valley
15. Tashme

Other areas within Canada

1. Kananaskis, Alberta
2. Chatham, Ontario
3. Petawawa, Ontario
4. Schreiber, Ontario
5. St. Thomas, Ontario
6. Toronto, Ontario
7. Hull, Quebec
8. Minto, New Brunswick
9. Amherst, Nova Scotia

In January of 1943, the Canadian government authorized the sale of all properties seized from the Japanese Canadians. Homes, cars, businesses and personal property left behind were sold for a paltry sum.

When the war finally ended, the Canadian government took action to remove all Japanese Canadians from British Columbia. They were forced to select between being deported to Japan or relocating in areas east of the Rocky Mountains. Four thousand

Japanese Canadians were deported before public protests finally ended the deportations.

Ironically, there were over 150,000 Japanese Americans residing in Hawaii during the internments on the United States mainland and in Canada. Of these, only 2,270 were actually interned according to the statistics compiled by the Japanese Cultural Center of Hawaii. This was primarily attributable to the fact that removing the Japanese Americans, who comprised one third of Hawaii's population at the time, would have had a devastating impact on the economy. Also, relocating these people to the mainland internment camps posed logistical difficulties.

Those who were interned were held at one of several camps that had opened up in Hawaii after December 7, 1941, or sent to the mainland. The interned group was primarily comprised of Japanese language teachers, Japanese newspaper editors, and officers of the Japanese Chamber of Commerce. There were also eight women who were interned. These women were students of Shinto and did not have full mastery of the English language. There was a Shinto priestess among them, and they were all subjected to interrogations and mistreatment.

There were seventeen camps situated in Hawaii, as listed below:

Kauai

1. Waimea Jail
2. Kalaheo Stockade
3. Wailua Jail
4. Lihue Plantation Gymnasium
5. Kauai Courthouse

Oahu

1. Honouliuli Internment Camp
2. Sand Island Detention Camp

3. US Immigration Station
4. Honolulu Police Department
5. Honolulu Military Police Station
6. Yokohama Specie Bank

Molokai

1. Kaunakakai Jail

Maui

1. Maui Jail, Haiku Military Camp

Lanai

1. Lanai Jail

Hawaii

1. Hilo Independent Japanese Language School
2. Waiakea Prison
3. Kilauea Military Camp

The Honouliuli Internment Camp was the largest camp and held 370 Japanese American internees in addition to 4,000 prisoners of war (POWs). Interestingly, the POWs received better treatment than the internees.

Although the possibility of Japanese American disloyalty was very remote, there was an incident that took place between December 7 and 13, 1941, which gave the public pause for thought. This instance became known as the Niihau Incident.

Following the attack on Pearl Harbor, Imperial Japanese Navy Air Service pilot Shigenori Nishikaichi, crash-landed his Mitsubishi Zero on the Hawaiian island of Niihau, located southwest of the island of Kauai. Prior to the attack, the Imperial Japanese Navy had mistakenly designated the island of Niihau as a safe, uninhabited location for damaged aircraft to land. Stranded pilots were instructed to wait on the island until they could be rescued by submarine. To the contrary, the tiny 48 square mile island was home to 180 Hawaiians and two Japanese families.

After landing on the island, Nishikaichi was relieved of his pistol and papers by a local Hawaiian named Hawila Kaleohano. Unable to communicate with the pilot, Kaleohano sent for Ishimatsu Shintani, a 60-year-old Japanese-born man who was married to a local Hawaiian woman, to help translate. After a brief conversation with Nishikaichi, Shintani departed without saying a word, forcing Kaleohano to send for another Japanese, 39-year-old Yoshio Harada. Yoshio and his wife Irene Umeno Harada were both nisei, born in Hawaii.

Nishikaichi informed the Haradas of what had taken place at Pearl Harbor and desperately asked to have his papers returned. Apparently, he had been warned that the papers, which included maps, radio codes and the Pearl Harbor attack plan, should by no means fall into hands of the Americans. The inhabitants of Niihau were unaware that the United States was now at war with Japan, and the Haradas decided that it would be prudent not to tell them. They asked Kaleohano to return the pilot's papers. When he refused, the Haradas decided to assist Nishikaichi in retrieving his papers and escaping.

By nightfall, word of the attack on Pearl Harbor had reached Niihau by radio. The pilot was questioned again, and it was determined that he should be taken to the island of Kauai by Niihau's landlord, Aylmer Robinson. Robinson lived on Kauai and made weekly visits to Niihau. Unbeknown to the Niihauans, newly imposed wartime restrictions had prohibited boat traffic across the 17-mile channel between Niihau and Kauai. Robinson was unable to return to Niihau as planned.

Nishikaichi was allowed to stay with the Haradas until he could be transported to Kauai. A guard was stationed outside the Harada residence to ensure that the pilot did not escape.

On December 12, Ishimatsu Shintani approached Kaleohano with $200 in cash, which he offered in exchange for the pilot's papers. Kaleohano refused and Shintani left, warning that there would be trouble. Later that evening, Harada and Nishikaichi overpowered the guard posted outside, acquired a shotgun and the pilot's pistol that were stored in a warehouse nearby, and proceeded to Kaleohano's house.

Unable to find him, they made their way to the pilot's downed plane to attempt to make contact with the Japanese military using the aircraft's radio. Unable to make contact, they managed to remove one of the two machine guns on board the plane and later set fire to the craft.

They then set fire to Kaleohano's house in a final effort to destroy Nishikaichi's papers. They were unaware that Kaleohano had given the pilot's papers to a relative for safekeeping.

On the morning of December 13, Nishikaichi and Harada captured two locals, Ben Kanahele and his wife Ella. They ordered Ben to find Kaleohano and kept Ella as a hostage to ensure that Ben followed through on the directive. Later that day, Ben and

Ella realized that the pilot and his companion were fatigued and turned on them. During the attack, Nishikaichi shot Ben three times. Despite being shot, Ben picked the pilot up and hurled him into a stone wall. Ella struck him on the head with a rock and Ben slit his throat with a hunting knife. Harada, witnessing the incident, turned the shotgun on himself and committed suicide.

When the Army rescue party from Kauai arrived on December 14, Irene Harada and Ishimatsu Shintani were taken into custody. Shintani was sent to an internment camp, where he remained for four years. Irene Harada, thought to be a Japanese spy, was imprisoned at the Wailua Jail on December 15, 1941. She was later transferred to the Honouliuli Internment Camp on Oahu where she remained until June of 1944. In an interview given to Patsy Sumie Saiki for her book, *Ganbare! An Example of Japanese Spirit* published in 2004, Irene asked, "My husband paid the penalty for his actions, whatever his motives were that last day. He gave his life for someone whom he hardly knew, but who was a human being before he was a friend or enemy. Is loyalty to a country stronger than kindness to a human being who is right there before you?"

Although the actions of Nishikaichi's abettors did demonstrate the potential for ethnic allegiance, the internments on the mainland resulted more from racism than a security risk posed by individuals of Japanese heritage.

Once the internment camps were officially closed, many of the internees did not have the means to return home. Although the United States government had transported these people to the camps, the responsibility of leaving the camp and traveling to the next destination rested with the individual.

For example, when Manzanar finally closed on November 21, 1945, the camp residents were each given $25 for a one-way train or bus ticket. Those who had less than $600 were provided with meals. Although many left the camp voluntarily, a significant number refused to leave because they had no place to go after losing everything when they were forcibly uprooted from their homes. As such, they had to be forcibly removed once again, this time from Manzanar. One hundred forty six Japanese Americans did not have an opportunity to leave the camp when it closed as they had died at Manzanar.

In an ironic twist, even as their families were interned in military style camps, many of the young nisei volunteered or were drafted to serve in the United States military.

Since the 1920s, the United States Navy refused to allow anyone of Japanese ancestry to serve, due to questions about their loyalty to the United States and the Empire of Japan. Following the attack on Pearl Harbor, all Japanese American men of draft age were classified as "4C," enemy aliens. This classification prevented them from enlisting in the armed forces entirely.

However, on February 1, 1943, President Roosevelt activated the 442nd Regimental Combat Team, an infantry regiment composed entirely of second generation Japanese American soldiers. Hawaii-born nisei made up about two-thirds of the regiment. The remaining one-third were nisei from the mainland. Only 1,208 nisei, less than 6 percent of eligible draft-age men, enlisted in the military voluntarily from the camps as a whole. The number was far short of the quota the War Department had set for itself in creating the all-nisei combat team. The Department was hoping for at least 2,000 initial volunteers.

In preparation for recruiting the nisei into an all-nisei combat regiment, the War Department and the War Relocation Authority joined forces to create a questionnaire they could use to evaluate the loyalty of the Japanese interned in the relocation camps. The form was informally known as the "loyalty questionnaire." The questions contained on the form focused on identifying family members, past residences, educational levels, language skills, religion, recreational activities, affiliations with associations, and family members and/or property in Japan. The questions were then carefully scored according to the degree of how American or Japanese each response appeared to be. For example, being fluent in Japanese, or belonging to a judo or kendo club would result in negative points. Being Christian, or belonging to the Boy Scouts of America would result in positive points.

Since these second generation Japanese men were required to fill out their forms as a part of the Selective Service process, refusing to comply would have resulted in being prosecuted for violating the Espionage Act. There were 19,963 military age second generation Japanese American men interned in the relocation camps. Of the six percent that had volunteered, approximately 800 had actually passed the loyalty tests and their physical examinations and were inducted into the original 442nd regiment.

Prior to the 442nd being mobilized, there was another nisei battalion composed largely of former members of the 298th and 299th Regiments of the Hawaii National Guard, designated as the 100th Infantry Battalion. Over 1,400 members of the Hawaii National Guard were young men of Japanese ancestry.

After the attack on Pearl Harbor on December 7th, the 298th and 299th Regiments of the Hawaii National Guard were federalized and ordered to defend the Hawaiian Islands against a potential invasion by Japanese forces. To take their place, the Hawaii Territorial Guard was created.

The Hawaii Territorial Guard was comprised of members from the University of Hawaii Army ROTC. This unit was made up of approximately 500 male students, 75 percent of whom were nisei. The Hawaii Territorial Guard members were issued Springfield .03 rifles and told to prepare for battle with Japanese paratroopers, who were rumored to be planning an invasion. They were ordered to guard government buildings, vital power stations and the shorelines of Honolulu. Fortunately, the invasion never took place.

Six weeks later, the Hawaii Territorial Guard was disbanded and reorganized without the nisei, who were now classified as enemy aliens.

The young nisei wanted to prove their loyalty and petitioned the military governor, General Delos C. Emmons, asking to serve their country in any capacity possible. A little over a month following the petition, they were granted the right to work with the Army Engineers. Although they were officially known as the Corps of Engineers Auxiliary, they were commonly known as the Varsity Victory Volunteers (The Triple-V).

The Varsity Victory Volunteers devoted the next 11 months to constructing warehouses, portable field huts, roads, bridges, bomb shelters and barbed wire fences in an attempt to help the United States with its war effort.

In the meantime, there was concern over whether the nisei members of the 298th and 299th Regiments could be trusted. These men were segregated and sent to the Schofield Barracks, nestled at the foot of the Waianae mountain range in Oahu, only 17 miles from Honolulu.

During the Battle of Midway in June of 1942, the nisei members of the 298th and 299th were sent to the Hawaiian Provisional Infantry Battalion and secretly shipped to the mainland on June 5th. When they landed in San Francisco, they were designated as the 100th Infantry Battalion and sent to North Africa in 1943. The 100th Infantry Battalion entered combat in Italy on September 26, 1943, while the 442nd was still being formed and trained.

It did not come as a surprise that most of the members of the Varsity Victory Volunteers volunteered to serve in the 442nd Regimental Combat Team. As a matter of fact, they were the first to be accepted into the unit. Seven Triple-V volunteers lost their lives in battle.

The 100th battalion combined with the 442nd on June 15, 1944.

The 442nd Regiment fought primarily in Europe during World War II, and their motto was "Go For Broke." It was derived from gambler's slang used in Hawaii, which meant that the player was risking it all on one effort to win big. It was an appropriate choice for the nisei of the 442nd, as they needed to put everything on the line to win big. They were fighting to win not only the war against the Germans in Europe but also the war against racial prejudice in the United States.

The 442nd Regimental Combat Team was the most decorated unit for its size and length of service in the entire history of the US military. The original regiment consisted of 4,000 men, which later grew to include 18,000 men. The 442nd ultimately earned 9,486

Purple Hearts, 21 Medals of Honor and an unprecedented seven Presidential Unit Citations.

***

In 1980, under mounting pressure from the Japanese American Citizens League and various redress organizations, President Jimmy Carter opened an investigation to determine whether the decision to put Japanese Americans into internment camps had been justified by the government. He appointed the Commission on Wartime Relocation and Internment of Civilians to investigate the camps. The Commission's report, titled *Personal Justice Denied*, found little evidence of Japanese disloyalty at the time and concluded that the incarceration had been the product of racism. The commission recommended that the government pay reparations to the survivors.

In 1988, President Ronald Reagan signed into law the Civil Liberties Act, which apologized for the internment on behalf of the United States government and authorized a payment of $20,000 to each individual camp survivor. The legislation admitted that government actions were based on "racial prejudice, war hysteria and a failure of political leadership."

Until February of 1945, the Allies engaged the Japanese in battle at sea and on foreign soil. On February 19, 1945, 30,000 marines landed on the southeast coast of Iwo Jima, bringing the war to Japan's front door for the first time.

The battle raged from February 19 to March 26, 1945 resulting in the capture of the island by US troops. The three airfields located on the island made Iwo Jima a target for the United States military, who wanted the airfields to serve as staging areas for future attacks on the Japanese mainland.

Anticipating the arrival of the United States forces, the Japanese Army, numbering 21,000, was heavily entrenched. They had established a concentrated network of bunkers, hidden artillery positions and 18 km (11 miles) of underground tunnels running throughout the island, which itself is only 3 km (2 miles) wide by 6 km (4 miles) long. The United States forces, on the other hand, relied on naval artillery and air support provided by United States Navy and Marine Corps aviators. Consequently, the Battle of Iwo Jima included some of the fiercest and bloodiest battles of the Pacific War to date.

When the first wave of Marines set foot on the island following the months of naval and air bombardment that had preceded the landing, they encountered 15-foot-high slopes of soft black volcanic ash. Iwo Jima is one of three small volcanic islands forming the Japanese Kazanretto (Volcano Islands) archipelago. The ash slowed their advancement and prevented them from digging foxholes to shield themselves from enemy fire. Taking advantage of the situation, Lieutenant General Tadamichi Kuribayashi waited patiently until the beach became crowded with Marines before unleashing his machine guns, mortars, and heavy artillery. Within minutes, the beach was transformed into a nightmarish bloodbath.

To make matters worse, the United States forces attempted to clear the bunkers with flamethrowers and grenades, but since they were connected by an elaborate tunnel system, Japanese troops were able to quickly reoccupy the bunkers, ready to fire again on the unsuspecting Marines.

Eventually, the Japanese forces ran out of supplies, food, and water, and as defeat seemed imminent, they launched a series of nighttime attacks on the American forces.

When the island was secured by the United States forces on March 26, of the 21,000 Japanese troops, 216 were taken as prisoners. Another 3,000 remained hidden in the extensive tunnel system and carried on fighting. By June, another 867 Japanese soldiers were captured and 1,602 were killed. Two Japanese soldiers, Yamakage Koufuku (山蔭光福兵長) and Matsudo Rikio (松戸利喜夫), held out, finally surrendering over five years later, on January 6, 1951! The others chose to commit ritual suicide rather than being captured. The Japanese called the soldiers who refused to surrender, *zanryu nipponhei* (residual Japanese soldiers).

Of the 70,000 United States forces, 5,900 were listed dead and 17,400 were wounded during the battle.

The next US advance on Japanese soil came on April 1, 1945, with the Battle of Okinawa. Codenamed Operation Iceberg, the fighting lasted until June 22, 1945 and was the most ferocious and bloodiest battles of World War II.

Not only did the Japanese use 77,000 army and navy personnel, they also relied on 39,000 native Okinawans, 24,000 of whom were drafted into the militia, known as *Boeitai*. The majority of the Okinawan Boeitai were just teenagers, the rest in their 30s and 40s.

Additionally, the Japanese Imperial Army used middle school boys known as *Tekketsu Kinnotai* on the front lines and drafted a group of female students into nursing units known as the *Himeyuri Corps* to care for the injured on the battlefields.

The Tekketsu Kinnotai (Iron and Blood Imperial Corps) consisted of 1,780 boys between the ages of 14 and 17. The military authorities forced them to "volunteer" as soldiers, leading guerilla operations and suicide bomb attacks against enemy tanks. Approximately half of these boys lost their lives during the battles.

The Himeyuri Corps was a group of 222 students and 18 teachers from the Okinawa Daiichi Women's High School and the Okinawa Shihan Women's School, who formed a nursing unit. They were mobilized by the Japanese Army on March 23, 1945. During the three-month-long Battle of Okinawa these students served on the front lines, performing surgeries and attending to the medical needs of the injured.

On June 18, 1945, the unit was ordered to be dissolved. In the week following the dissolution order, approximately 80 percent of the girls and their teachers were killed. Those who did not die on the front lines committed suicide, in various ways, because of their fear of being systematically raped by United States soldiers. Some of the women threw themselves off cliffs, while others killed themselves with hand grenades given to them by Japanese soldiers.

Okinawa is home to an ethnically diverse group of people. Previously known as the Ryukyu Kingdom, it became a Japanese domain in the early part of the Meiji period, placing it under the direct leadership of Japan. At that time, native Okinawans were treated as second-class citizens by the Japanese government and made to suffer. During the Pacific War, they were sacrificed by the Japanese military.

Prior to the United States' main landing in Okinawa on April 1st, 1945 there had been two earlier landings. The first took place on March 26 when soldiers from the 77th Infantry set foot on the Kerama Islands, 24 km (15 miles) west of Okinawa. The American forces suffered minimal losses with only 27 dead and 81 wounded while the Japanese losses numbered 650, both dead and captured. This first battle afforded the United States' fleet the protected anchorage it needed to help launch the rest of the attacks.

The second landing took place on March 31, when the US Marines came onshore at Keiseshima, located 13 km (8 miles) west of Okinawa's capital city of Naha.

Finally, on April 1, 1945, the Marines landed on Hagushi Beach located in Yomitan, Okinawa. The Kadena and Yomitan airbases fell rather easily within hours of the landing. Of the 19,000 Marines that were part of the landing, only two were killed and nine wounded. The US forces were surprised by the lack of Japanese resistance and soon found droves of native Okinawans, who had been suffering at the hands of the Japanese, surrendering to the Americans. Most had leprosy and showed signs of severe malnutrition.

April 2 saw the expected fighting at night, which the Japanese were known for. However, by dawn's early light, the Americans were surprised to see that the battlefield was littered with the corpses of native Okinawans.

On April 6, the Japanese military, who had been quiet up until this point, finally struck. The *Kamikaze* launched an attack on the fleet in an effort to strand the American troops on shore. During the attack, 900 aircraft sank 11 ships and damaged 22. Within the next two weeks, 2,000 Japanese planes attacked the American fleet, killing 5,000 sailors.

As the fighting continued, the Japanese concentrated their defenses on the Shuri Line, a 13 km (8 mile) path stretching from Yonabaru on the east coast through tortuous mountain ridges near Shuri Castle and extending to the Port of Naha on Okinawa's west coast.

As the United States' forces attempted to overtake the Japanese forces along the Shuri Line, they were subjected to heavy rains beginning on May 22. The rain continued daily for weeks and impeded the Americans' advances as the troops got mired in the mud. During this time, the Japanese Air Force launched its greatest aerial offensive. It dispatched 896 kamikaze raids inflicting serious damage on the American ships. At the same time, the Ie, the Yontan and the Kadena airfields were bombed.

By May 29, US troops had captured Naha and Yonabaru, setting the stage for the encirclement of Shuri in the center. However, on May 24, General Mitsuru Ushijima had already decided to withdraw from Shuri and move his forces to the south in an effort to further prolong the battle and inflict additional losses on the American forces.

The Japanese forces abandoned Shuri on May 29 leaving behind small units to serve as the rear guard for the withdrawing troops. By May 31, the Americans had successfully captured Shuri. In the process, Shuri was levelled and left in complete ruin. The Japanese army was decimated with over 70,000 killed in action. Only nine Japanese soldiers had been captured by the US forces because they were either badly wounded or unconscious. Very few Japanese soldiers were captured because the Japanese soldier was expected to fight until he was killed. Those soldiers who were wounded either died from their wounds or were returned to the front lines to fight until they were killed.

A new Japanese defense line was established from Gushichan to Itoman. On June 1, the American forces launched their final attack. On June 4, the Naha Airfield was captured and a small naval force led by Admiral Minoru Ota was wiped out. Admiral Ota later committed suicide by *hara-kiri* (a ritual suicide by disembowelment with a sword, formerly practiced in Japan by samurai as an honorable alternative to disgrace or execution).

By June 17, the United States forces penetrated and held all the major positions along the Gushichan-Itoman defensive line. The fighting became truly maddening as every remaining Japanese soldier was commanded to fight to the death. Thousands of Japanese were holed up in caves around Madeera and Makabe defending fanatically, forcing the fighting to continue until June 21, during which time the survivors were eliminated and the last pocket of resistance was secured.

But the story does not end there. Unlike the Battle of Iwo Jima, which was uninhabited, Okinawa had a civilian population of approximately 300,000 citizens. More than one quarter of Okinawa's population were killed during the battle.

It was common for Japanese soldiers to disguise themselves as native Okinawans. Given the number of civilians that were pressed into service by the Japanese army, the American troops often found it difficult to distinguish civilians from soldiers and fired indiscriminately into Okinawan houses. Many civilians hid out in caves in an effort to protect themselves from enemy fire. Countless Okinawan families hiding from the United States' troops committed mass suicide. The civilians were told that if they were captured by American soldiers, the women would be raped and the men would be run over by tanks.

At Chibichiri Gama, a cave located in Yomitan, the cave floor is littered with knives, syringes and bones. It was here that 85 Okinawan civilians were instructed by the Japanese army to take their own lives rather than being captured by the Americans. Half of those killed were under the age of 12.

Further, the Japanese army showed complete indifference to civilian safety and used them as human shields or just outright murdered them. The military confiscated food from the civilians and killed those suspected of hiding food. The army also executed approximately 1,000 civilians who conversed in their native tongue, in an effort to suppress spying.

The allied offensive in Japan continued in the form of a series of bombing raids. Starting with the Doolittle Raid in April of 1942, the air raids continued through 1945 and killed an estimated 900,000 people.

The Doolittle Raid was headed by Lieutenant Colonel James H. Doolittle and took place during the morning of April 18, 1942. Sixteen B-25 bombers took off from the aircraft carrier USS Hornet situated 600 miles away from the Japanese coast and launched attacks on Tokyo, Nagoya, Osaka, and Kobe.

Although the damage was insignificant compared to subsequent attacks, it left the Japanese feeling vulnerable.

In September of 1943, the Japanese military set up an absolute national zone of defense—an area which had to be defended at all costs. The zone's perimeter stretched from the Marianas and Caroline Islands to western New Guinea out to the Banda and Flores Seas. When Saipan, the most important strategic point within the zone, fell on July of 1944, a decision was made to transfer the Imperial Palace, the army headquarters, and other important government departments to the town of Matsushiro located in the Nagano prefecture.

The plan was to construct a massive underground bunker complex capable of withstanding B-29 bombings. It was decided that the complex would be located underneath several mountains, and the facilities would be interlinked by a series of underground tunnels. The Imperial General Headquarters and the Palace were to be located under Mount Maizuru; the military communications under Mount Saijo; government agencies, the NHK (Japan's largest broadcasting organization), and central telephone facilities under Mount Zozan; the residences of the Imperial Family under Mount Minakami; and the Imperial Sanctuary under Mount Kobo.

Construction of the bunkers began on November 11, 1944 and continued until Japan's surrender on August 15, 1945. At the time of surrender, construction was 75% complete with 63,040 sq. ft. of floor space excavated. In total, 7,000 Koreans and 3,000 Japanese laborers worked three eight-hour shifts and later two twelve-hour shifts to build the complex at a cost of ¥200,000,000.

Although the bunker was never used as originally intended, it was utilized by other agencies after the war.

On March 9, 1945, American warplanes launched the firebombing of Tokyo by dropping 2,000 tons of incendiary bombs on the city within 48 hours. The attack incinerated 16 square miles in and around the Japanese capital and killed an estimated 130,000 Japanese civilians. To date, this attack is considered the single worst firestorm in recorded history.

Japan's military and civil defenses were quite ineffective with regard to defending against these Allied attacks. There weren't enough fighter aircraft and anti-aircraft guns available to defend Japan's home islands. Furthermore, the aircraft and guns that were available were unable to attack the high altitudes at which the B-29s were capable of flying. Japan's fuel shortages, inadequate pilot training, and lack of coordination between its military units also contributed to the success of the American bombings.

The Japanese firefighters were not adequately trained and lacked the equipment necessary to deal with the resulting fires. The firefighting forces had few full-time professional firefighters and relied primarily on volunteers.

Although air raid drills had been held in Tokyo and Osaka since 1928 and local governments were required to provide civilians with manuals that explained how to respond to air attacks, very few air raid shelters had been constructed for civilians before the Pacific War.

Moreover, due to their design, Japanese cities were highly vulnerable to damage from fire bombings. Urban areas were typically congested and most buildings were constructed from highly flammable materials, such as paper and wood. Industries were located in residential areas, which made it impossible for the Americans to avoid damaging civilian residences when attacking the industrial and military facilities.

Despite suffering crippling damage to property and huge losses of human life, Japan continued to fight on. The events which would bring the country to its knees were only four months away.

On August 6, 1945, an American B-29 bomber named the Enola Gay dropped the world's first atomic bomb over the city of Hiroshima, the largest city in the Chugoku region of western

Honshu. The city was an embarkation port, industrial center, and home to Field Marshal Shunroku Hata's Second General Army headquarters. Hiroshima also housed large stockpiles of military supplies; therefore, it was chosen as the first target. At the time of the attack, Hiroshima's population was approximately 350,000.

At 8:15 a.m., a 64 kg uranium bomb detonated 580 meters (1,900 feet) above Hiroshima. The explosion destroyed 90 percent of the city and instantly killed 80,000 people. Tens of thousands more would die later from radiation exposure.

Shukkeien Garden, which was constructed in 1620 just after the completion of Hiroshima Castle, is a very popular attraction in Hiroshima today. The shrunken scenery garden consisting of valleys, mountains, waterfalls, tea houses, and forests enjoys over 180,000 visitors annually.

The garden is important because it is located only three-quarters of a mile from the hypocenter of the atomic bomb. All of the structures in the garden were destroyed and the vegetation burned with the exception of one tree, which withstood the blast. Those who were injured by the bomb took refuge in the garden and died there. Their remains were interred within the garden.

News of the devastation in Hiroshima was slow to reach other areas of Japan. In Tokyo, the operator of the Japan Broadcasting Corporation noticed that the Hiroshima station had unexpectedly gone off the air. He tried to reestablish his program by using another telephone line, but that too failed. Approximately 20 minutes later, the Tokyo railroad telegraph center realized that the main line telegraph just north of Hiroshima had stopped working. Unofficial and confusing reports began filtering in from small railway stops within 16 km (10 miles) of the city indicating that a terrible explosion had taken place in Hiroshima. These reports were later transmitted to the headquarters of the Imperial Japanese Army General Staff.

Several military bases tried repeatedly to contact the Army Control Station in Hiroshima. The complete silence prompted them to send a young officer to fly immediately to Hiroshima to survey the damage and return to Tokyo with his findings.

Sixteen hours later, in an announcement made by President Truman, Tokyo received its first indication that Hiroshima had been destroyed by a new type of bomb.

Three days later, on August 9, 1945, a US Army Air Force B-29 bomber named Bockscar, flown by Major Charles W. Sweeney's crew, dropped an implosion-type nuclear weapon over the city of Nagasaki.

Nagasaki was one of the largest seaports in Japan and the center for industries producing military supplies, weapons, ammunition and vehicles. This made the city the target of the second nuclear bomb to be used in a war.

At 7:50 a.m., Japanese time, an air raid alert was heard in Nagasaki. However, by 8:30 a.m. an all clear was given and the people returned to their daily activities. At 10:53 a.m., two B-29 Superfortresses were spotted flying over the city but no alarm was sounded as the Japanese assumed that the planes were merely on a reconnaissance mission. At 11:01 a.m., the Fat Man, a 6.4 kg (14 pound) plutonium weapon, was dropped on the city and exploded 47 seconds later above a tennis court located halfway between Mitsubishi Steel and Arms Works and the Nagasaki Arsenal.

The explosion generated temperatures of 3,900°C (7,050 °F) and winds over 1,000 km/h (620 mph). Of the 7,500 employees who worked at the Mitsubishi plant, 6,200 were killed. Casualty rates vary drastically due to the number of undocumented foreign workers and military personnel in transit. However, it is estimated that 35,000 to 40,000 people were killed and 60,000 were injured at the time of the bombing. In the days and months that followed, more people died from exposure to radiation.

Death came in various forms after the bombs were dropped on Hiroshima and Nagasaki. Many residents were crushed under the rubble of their homes and businesses. Their skeletons could be seen in the debris, and ashes were scattered to almost 1,500 meters (1,650 yards) from the epicenters of the explosions. Several people were able to walk considerable distances after the detonation before they collapsed and died.

Others, who were not killed immediately, died within one to two weeks after the bombings. They suffered from vomiting, and bloody and watery diarrhea. The floors of numerous aid stations were covered with vomit and bloody feces. During this same period, countless people died from internal injuries, burns sustained from the fires, or from the infrared radiation caused by the detonation of the bombs.

Within four to six weeks after the bombs were dropped, people began to die from what was termed bone marrow syndrome. They developed a condition known as purpura, which is the appearance of red or purple colored spots on the skin caused by internal bleeding. The bone marrow syndrome caused extremely low white blood cell counts and almost a complete absence of platelets required to prevent bleeding.

The atomic bombs dropped on the cities of Hiroshima and Nagasaki obliterated not only the war industry but also many innocent lives as well. Those who survived the blasts were scarred for life both physically and emotionally.

The Japanese soon coined a term to describe those who had survived the nuclear bomb attacks. The term was *hibakusha*, meaning explosion-affected people.

Perhaps the most famous of the hibakusha were the Hiroshima Maidens. The maidens were twenty-five young women who were seriously disfigured by the atomic bomb. Their faces were heavily scarred by the burns, and their limbs were so damaged that they never properly healed. These young women were stigmatized after the war; some were hidden from the public by their parents, stared at when they ventured outside, unwanted by employers, and rejected as potential wives for fear they were genetically damaged.

Reverend Kiyoshi Tanimoto, a Methodist minister, himself a bombing survivor, created a charitable foundation to help the victims of Hiroshima. Tanimoto had gained some fame in the United States as the subject of the 1946 book titled *Hiroshima* by Pulitzer Prize-winning author John Hersey. His fame enabled him to enlist the help of several American journalists in creating the Hiroshima Peace Centre Foundation. Among the foundation's most notable members were John Hersey, Pearl S. Buck, Norman Cousins, and Reverend Marvin Green.

In an effort to raise funds for the foundation, Reverend Tanimoto went on extensive speaking tours in the United States. He even appeared on the popular television program *This Is Your Life*, during which he and his family were placed in the uncomfortable position of meeting with Captain Robert A. Lewis, the co-pilot of the Enola Gay, which had dropped the atomic bomb on Hiroshima.

Norman Cousins was the editor of *The Saturday Review*, an

American weekly magazine established in 1924, which undertook a project called Moral Adoptions. The project began with an appeal to its readers in 1949 to adopt from a distance approximately 400 children in Hiroshima who were orphaned as a result of the atomic bomb explosion.

The Moral Adoptions project resulted in the building of new orphanages and the expansion of existing ones throughout Hiroshima. The adoptive parents in the United States corresponded with their adopted children in Japan and contributed to the support of the orphanages. Through their support, the children were able to receive special educational training and the majority of them went on to college or vocational schools. The Moral Adoptions project was administered by the Hiroshima Peace Centre Foundation.

In 1952, the Hiroshima Peace Center Associates raised funds enabling the Hiroshima Maidens to have plastic surgery in Tokyo and Osaka. Unfortunately, plastic surgery in Japan was not as advanced as it was in the United States and the results proved to be unsatisfactory. Consequently, the foundation tried to find a way to get the maidens to the United States. Two doctors, William Maxwell Hitzig and Arthur Barsky of Mount Sinai Hospital in New York, agreed to supervise the medical operations. On May 5, 1955, the young women along with three Hiroshima surgeons departed for the United States. The three surgeons who accompanied the maidens traveled to the United States to study American plastic surgery techniques.

There were a total of 138 surgeries performed on the 25 women over a period of 18 months. One of the girls, Hiroko Tasaka, came to be known as the "champion surgery girl" because she endured 13 operations, more than any of the other girls in the program. Another girl, Tomoko Nakabayashi, died due to cardiac arrest while undergoing reconstructive surgery on May 24, 1956. The doctors declared that the death was due to complications during the operation and not as a result of being exposed to radiation from the bomb blast.

On March 31, 2016, the Japanese government certified 174,080 living hibakusha. The average age of these citizens was 75 at the time. Their children and grandchildren were called hibakusha nisei and hibakusha sansei. They too were ostracized, because they purportedly possessed the damaged DNA of their lineage.

# Photos

A.  Japanese Imperial Army in Manchuria.

B.  Kempeitai Headquarters in Nanking, China.

C.  Kempeitai Officer.

D.  Explosion of the USS Shaw's forward magazine during the attack on Pearl Harbor. The ship was later repaired and served in the Pacific throughout World War II.

E.  Manzanar Relocation Center, California (winter of 1943).

F.  Interned Japanese American Sumiko Shigematsu (standing at left) supervises fellow internees working at sewing machines at Manzanar Relocation Center (1943).

G.  A Japanese American veteran, dressed in his WWI uniform, reports for his WWII internment. Santa Anita Park Assembly Center, Arcadia, California (April 5, 1942).

H.  Injured female survivor of the Nagasaki atomic bombing. (September 1945).

I.  Aftermath of World War II atomic bombing in a suburb four miles outside of central Nagasaki City, Japan.

J.  Tokyo's shanty town, where post-World War II homeless Japanese set up housekeeping in small huts amid the ruins (September 26, 1945).

K.  Food stall in post-World War II Tokyo.

L.  Homeless Japanese in Tokyo.

M.  Analog for Japanese PURPLE (MAGIC) code (Pearl Harbor, Hawaii).

N.  The Japanese Kaiten ( Pearl Harbor, Hawaii).

O.  Hiroshima Prisoner of War Sub-Camp No.4 Memorial (Onomichi).

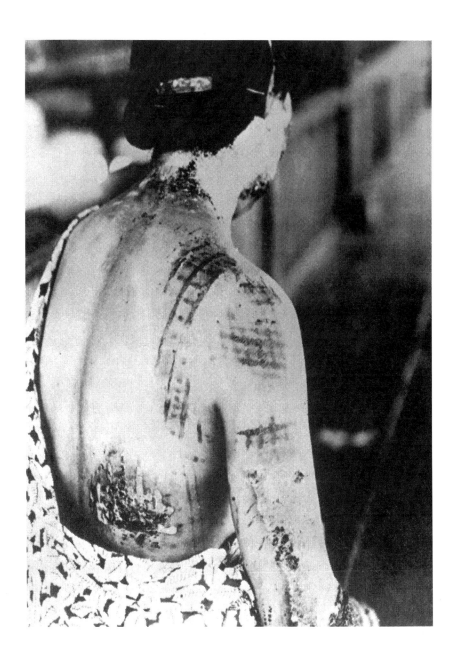

# JAPANESE SURRENDER

On July 26, 1945, United States President Harry Truman, United Kingdom Prime Minister Winston Churchill, and Republic of China President Chiang Kai-shek drew up a proclamation defining the terms for Japan's unconditional surrender. This was done midway through the Potsdam Conference. Although the Chinese leader was not actually present at the conference, communication was kept up with the Chinese Nationalist Party (KMT) throughout. Soviet leader Joseph Stalin also attended the Potsdam Conference but did not sign the declaration. Known as the Potsdam Declaration, the document stated that if Japan did not surrender, it would face "prompt and utter destruction."

Japan, on the other hand, had its own terms and conditions for surrender. The terms optimistically stipulated that: (1) Japan must retain its emperor, (2) There would be no Allied occupation of the Japanese mainland, (3) Japan would disarm itself, and (4) Japan would try its own war criminals.

However, early in 1945, it was clear to Emperor Hirohito that Japan's chance for a military victory was very slim. Along with members of the Supreme Council and various elder statesmen, the emperor began exploring possible terms for a Japanese surrender.

Since the early 1930s, the Japanese government had been dominated by the military but still retained a few civilian ministers. The Supreme Council was made up of the Prime Minister, the Minister of Foreign Affairs, the Minister of the Army, the Minister of the Navy, and the Chiefs of Staff of the Army and the Navy.

The Supreme Council was deadlocked over how to achieve their desired terms. Those that opted for peace favored pursuing these terms with the Soviet Union acting as an intermediary between

Japan and the United States. Those that supported war pushed for a final decisive battle that would force the United States to accept the Japanese terms for peace. Unable to reach a final decision, the Japanese government decided to pursue both avenues at the same time. Foreign Minister Togo was permitted to approach the Soviet Union while preparations for the final decisive battle, dubbed Operation Ketsu-Go, went forward. Given Japan's shortages in resources and technology, Operation Ketsu-Go was not intended to prevent an American amphibious invasion but to make it so costly that the United States would be more willing to negotiate.

The plan divided the Japanese home territory into seven zones where the final decisive battles would be fought and involved three distinct phases. Phase I focused on utilizing the special attack forces of the Imperial Air Force and the Imperial Navy to attempt to destroy as many American navy aircraft carriers as possible. Phase II of the plan would be put into play when the American amphibious forces approached within range of the homeland air bases. The strategy was to deploy the entire air combat squad on continuous day and night assaults in an attempt to disrupt the United States' landing plans. The primary targets of Japan's attacks were to be the troop and equipment transports. Phase III of the plan involved using the Imperial Army to attack the American forces if they succeeded in landing on the mainland.

What the Supreme Council did not know was that the Soviets were preparing to attack the Japanese forces in Manchuria and Korea in accordance with an agreement Russia had secretly made with the United States and the United Kingdom at the Tehran and Yalta Conferences. This eliminated any hope of trying to end the war through peaceful negotiation.

By the end of World War II, Japan had persevered through eight years of war, taking into account their participation in the Second Sino-Japanese War which began in 1937. The country lay in ruins and with over three million dead. Today, one questions why the Japanese held on to the belief of fighting to the end and not surrendering.

Perhaps part of the answer can be found in *Bushido,* the samurai code of conduct. Bushido, or the way of the warrior, focused on the moral values of the samurai and included frugality, loyalty, martial arts mastery, and honor until death.

In the mid-nineteenth century, however, Bushido had been adopted as a way of providing ethical training for Japanese society as a whole, in which the emperor became the focus of loyalty and sacrifice. Following the Meiji Restoration (1868 - 1912), Bushido contributed to the rise of Japanese nationalism and strengthened civilian morale during the Sino-Japanese War and World War II.

During the Pacific War, very few Japanese actually surrendered and were taken prisoner. This was due to the fact that the Japanese soldiers fought until they were killed or committed suicide. As the war approached its last desperate months, Japanese civilians also adopted this ideology of honor until death. American troops in Saipan reported seeing mothers clutching their babies in their arms and hurling themselves off cliffs rather than being taken prisoner. The Japanese garrison in Saipan was 30,000 strong and yet there were virtually no survivors. Approximately 22,000 civilians also died.

Honor until death was even more evident within Japan's kamikaze pilots who committed the ultimate sacrifice for their country and their emperor by smashing their planes, packed with explosives, into enemy warships.

However, planes were not the only suicide vehicles used by the Japanese Special Attack Units. As the war turned more unfavorable for Japan, the Navy developed the Shinyo suicide boats, Kaiten submarines, and Fukuryu suicide divers, or human mines.

The Shinyo suicide boats were swift motorboats equipped with two anti-ship rockets mounted on launchers located on either side of the craft and bow-mounted explosives that could be detonated upon impact or by triggering a manual switch from within the driver's compartment. During the war, there were approximately 6,200 Shinyo produced. Four hundred of these craft were shipped to Okinawa and Taiwan (Fermosa), while the remainder were stored on the coast of Japan in preparation for the final defense of the home islands.

The Kaiten were essentially suicide torpedoes used between 1944 and 1945. The torpedo was equipped with a small cockpit, a periscope, and controls for steering, speed, and depth. It was powered by a 550 horsepower engine and carried a 3,000 pound warhead. Like the Shinyo, the explosives could either be detonated upon impact or by an electrical switch inside of the cockpit. The Japanese Navy used approximately 100 Kaiten during the war killing 96 Kaiten pilots (16 in training alone) and sunk only one US Navy ship, the USS Mississinewa in November of 1944. One merchant ship, the SS Canada Victory was also sunk by a Kaiten torpedo and the USS Underhill was severely damaged.

The Fukuryu suicide divers or human mines were just that—men in diving suits who were assigned to carry an explosive charge beneath a ship or landing craft and detonate it. Japan had planned to train 6,000 men for these missions. By August 15, 1945 only 1,000 diving suits were ready and none of the attack mines had been completed. Several deaths occurred during training due to malfunctions. When Japan surrendered, only 1,200 men had actually been trained as Fukuryu.

Although Japan is chiefly credited with masterminding the kamikaze suicide attacks, Axis and Allied pilots had also deliberately crashed their planes into enemy targets after suffering severe damage. These early attacks were motivated by the pilots' desire not to be captured and wanting to inflict as much damage to the enemy as possible, since the planes were going to crash anyway.

For Japan, the formation of the kamikaze suicide squads was an act of desperation after suffering irreparable damage during the aircraft carrier battles of 1942, particularly during the Battle of Midway. During that specific battle, the Imperial Japanese Navy lost as many air crewmen in a single day as their pre-war training program had produced in a year. Consequently, the Japanese military was unable to assemble a large number of aircraft carriers with well-trained crews to prevent the Allied advancement.

According to sources, Captain Motoharu Okamura was the first officer to conduct an investigation into the plausibility and mechanisms of suicide attacks, on June 15, 1944. In August of 1944, an announcement was made in the media that a flight instructor named Takeo Tagata was training pilots in Taiwan for suicide missions. On October 25, 1944, during the Battle of the Leyte Gulf, the Japanese officially deployed the kamikaze (divine wind) suicide bombers against American warships for the first time. As a result of the attack, seven carriers and 40 other ships were hit by the Kamikaze Special Attack Force. Five of the ships hit actually sunk, 23 were heavily damaged and 12 were moderately damaged.

These early successes prompted the Japanese military to increase their kamikaze squadrons. Many of the pilots were volunteers, who believed that their death would pay the debt they owed and show the love they had for their families, friends and the emperor. After the Japanese military's adoption of the kamikaze tactic, newspapers and books ran advertisements, articles and stories regarding the suicide bombers in an effort to aid in recruitment and support the program. Publishers played up the idea that the kamikaze would be enshrined at the Yasukuni Shrine and ran exaggerated stories of kamikaze bravery. Many Japanese believed that it was a special honor to be enshrined at Yasukuni because the emperor visited the shrine twice a year to pay homage. Yasukuni is the only shrine in Japan that deifies common men. There were even fairy tales for little children that promoted the kamikaze tactic.

While many stories were falsified, some were actually true. There was a popular story about a sergeant major Kiyu Ishikawa who saved a Japanese ship when he crashed his plane into a torpedo that an American submarine had launched. He was posthumously promoted to second lieutenant by the emperor and was enshrined at Yasukuni. Stories like these, which showed the kind of praise and honor death produced, encouraged young Japanese to volunteer for the Special Attack Corps and instilled a desire in the youth to die as a kamikaze.

While it is commonly perceived that volunteers signed up in droves for kamikaze missions, it has also been contended that there was extensive coercion and peer pressure involved in recruiting soldiers for the sacrifice. Interestingly, 11 of the 1,036 kamikaze pilots who died in attacks that originated from Chiran and other Japanese air bases during the Battle of Okinawa were Koreans.

Ceremonies were carried out as the kamikaze pilots prepared to depart on their final missions. The pilots shared ceremonial cups of sake or water known as *mizu no sakazuki.* The kamikaze who were army officers took their swords with them in their planes. Like all servicemen, the kamikaze pilots wore the traditional *senninbari,* a belt of a thousand stitches given to them by their mothers, sisters or wives. The senninbari was a strip of cloth that measured approximately six inches wide and three or four feet, or more, in length and served as an amulet, a part of Shinto culture.

The kamikaze pilots also composed and read death poems, a tradition stemming from the samurai who did it before committing *seppuku,* a form of Japanese ritual suicide by disembowelment. Pilots carried prayers from their families and were given military decorations. They were escorted by other pilots whose function was to protect the kamikaze pilots until they reached their destination and to report on the results. Some of these escort pilots were themselves later sent out on their own kamikaze missions.

The pilots were subjected to the *Tokkotai* (special attack force) pilot training program, which consisted of incredibly strenuous training coupled with cruel and torturous corporal punishment as a daily routine. This brutal training was justified by the idea that it would instill a fighting spirit in the soldiers. However, daily beatings and corporal punishment eliminated patriotism among many pilots.

Pilots were given a manual which detailed how they were supposed to think, prepare, and attack. From this manual, pilots were told to "attain a high level of spiritual training" and to "keep their health in the very best condition." These things, among others, were meant to put the pilot into the mindset in which he would be mentally ready to die.

*"When you eliminate all thoughts about life and death, you will be able to totally disregard your earthly life. This will also enable you to concentrate your attention on eradicating the enemy with unwavering determination, meanwhile reinforcing your excellence in flight skills."*
— excerpt from a kamikaze pilot's manual

Kamikaze pilots who were unable to complete their mission either due to mechanical failure or from being intercepted were stigmatized in the years following the war. However, as time wore on, many criticized the nationalist portrayal of kamikaze pilots as noble soldiers willing to sacrifice their lives for the country. One such person was the Tokyo newspaper *Yomiuri Shimbun* Editor-in-Chief, Tsuneo Watanabe. He wrote, "It's all a lie that they left filled with braveness and joy, crying, 'Long live the emperor!' They were sheep at a slaughterhouse. Everybody was looking down and tottering. Some were unable to stand up and were carried and pushed into the plane by maintenance soldiers."

The Japanese people had been indoctrinated from an early age to revere the emperor as a living god. They were taught that war was an act that would purify the self, the nation, and the entire world. Viewed within this framework, the supreme sacrifice of life itself was regarded as the purest of all accomplishments. They were reminded again and again not to live life in shame as a prisoner. Instead, die and leave no disgraceful crime behind you.

These attitudes, which formed the unique Japanese consciousness, were not only based on Bushido but also attributed to the teachings of *Shinto*, the Japanese ethnic religion, which dates back to the sixth century. Shinto teaches that certain deeds create a kind of ritual impurity, which requires cleansing. Purification rites (*harae*) are a vital part of the Shinto religion and are performed on a daily, weekly, seasonal, lunar and annual basis.

During the Meiji period, the government declared Shinto to be the state religion in which everyone could be united. Shinto priests became state officials, and major shrines received funding from the government. The religion's creation myths were used to nurture an emperor cult and Japanese political, social, military and religious institutions centered themselves around the figure of the emperor, who was seen as an icon of everything good, pure and holy.

The Japanese term for emperor is *tenno*, which means heavenly sovereign. According to mythology, Japan's first Emperor Jimmu was the descendant of the Sun Goddess Amaterasu. She is a part of the Japanese myth cycle and also a major deity of the Shinto religion. It is commonly accepted that all of the emperors who have reigned over Japan for more than 2,000 years have descended from Amaterasu.

While Bushido attributed to the rise of Japanese nationalism, Shinto was responsible for further strengthening it. In 1890, the *Imperial Rescript on Education* was issued requiring students to ritually recite its oath to "offer yourselves courageously to the State and protect the Imperial family."

But there was more to it than just the average Japanese citizen's fanatical devotion to their emperor, the Shinto doctrine, and the codes of bushido.

In his book entitled *The Faraway War: Personal Diaries of the Second World War in Asia and The Pacific* published in 2006, Professor Richard Aldrich of Nottingham University maintained that the American policy of not taking any prisoners in certain parts of the Pacific Theater made it less likely for the Japanese to surrender. Professor Aldrich based his assertion on first-hand accounts contained in the numerous diaries he gathered from men and women across the Pacific War front. Details of the way in which Japanese prisoners of war were treated came not only from military personnel but also from ordinary people. Aldrich also examined the personal diaries of some of the more celebrated figures of the time, including Arthur Evelyn St. John Waugh, Charles Lindbergh, Harry Truman, and Joyce Grenfell.

In discussing the dairy of Charles Lindbergh, Professor Aldrich talked about a conversation Mr. Lindberg had with a group of senior officers during one of his visits to the Far East. Mr. Lindberg had commented that "very few Japanese seemed to be taken prisoner."

"Oh, we could take more if we wanted to," one of the officers replied. "But our boys don't like to take prisoners."

"It doesn't encourage the rest to surrender when they hear of their buddies being marched out on the flying field and machine-guns turned loose on them."

The Australian troops were also merciless, according to Professor Aldrich. He quoted the 1943 diary of Eddie Stanton, an Australian stationed at Goodenough Island in the Solomon Sea. "Japanese are still being shot all over the place," he wrote. "The necessity for capturing them has ceased to worry anyone. Nippo soldiers are just so much machine-gun practice. Too many of our soldiers are tied up guarding them."

Surrendering as an individual may have been one thing but surrendering as a country was something quite different. Until August 9, 1945, even after the nuclear devastation of Hiroshima, Japan's Supreme Council still insisted on its four conditions for surrender, the most important of which was the retention of the emperor. At 4:00 a.m. that day, Tokyo received news that the Soviet Union had broken the Neutrality Pact, declared war on Japan, and launched an invasion of Manchuria. On the same day, a second nuclear bomb was dropped on the city of Nagasaki.

On August 12, the emperor informed the Imperial family of his decision to surrender. On August 14, hidden inside a bunker located on the palace compound, Emperor Hirohito recorded his announcement, which was broadcast to the Japanese nation the next day despite an attempted coup d'état by militarists opposed to the surrender.

The coup d'état attempt, known as the Kyujo Incident, took place after midnight on August 14, 1945. It was an attempt undertaken by the Staff Office of the Ministry of War of Japan and a group from the Imperial Guard of Japan. The leader of the rebellion was Major Kenji Hatanaka.

It was said that Hatanaka and his group wanted to prevent Japan from surrendering as they were uncertain of whether the Imperial system would still be maintained under the conditions of the Potsdam Declaration.

Hatanaka, Captain Shigetaro Uehara, and Lieutenant Colonel Jiro Shiizaki went to the office of Lieutenant General Takeshi Mori after midnight to persuade him to join their cause. When he refused, they killed him and used his official stamp to authorize a false set of orders, which would have enabled an increase in the number of the forces occupying the Imperial Palace and the Imperial Household Ministry. They intended to place the emperor under house arrest and confiscate the recording, which was locked in a small safe in the grand chamberlain's office.

The rebels managed to disarm the palace police and block all the entrances. They captured and detained eighteen people, including Ministry staff and NHK workers sent to record the surrender speech. The rebels then spent several hours unsuccessfully searching for the Imperial Household Minister, Sotaro Ishiwata, the Lord of the Privy Seal, Koichi Kido, and the recordings. Fortunately, the two men were hiding in a large chamber beneath the Imperial Palace and remained undiscovered. During the siege of the Imperial Palace nearly all of the telephone wires were cut, severing communications between the captives on the palace grounds and the outside world.

Unable to find the recordings and facing certain failure, Hatanaka pleaded with Tatsuhiko Takashima, the Chief of Staff of the Eastern District Army, to be given at least ten minutes on the air on NHK radio, to explain to the people of Japan what he was trying to accomplish and why. His request was refused. Just before 5:00 a.m. Hatanaka forcefully entered the NHK studios wielding a pistol. He tried desperately to convince the staff to provide him with airtime allowing him to explain his actions. Approximately an hour later, Hatanaka and his rebels finally gave up.

Shizuichi Tanaka, a general in the Imperial Japanese Army and the acting commander of the 1st Imperial Guards Division, went to the Imperial Palace after learning of the siege. There he confronted the rebellious officers, reprimanding them for acting contrary to the spirit of the Japanese Army. He succeeded in convincing them to return to their barracks.

By 8:00 a.m. the coup was crushed and Hatanaka rode through the streets on his motorcycle accompanied by Shiizaki on horseback, tossing leaflets that explained their motives and their actions. Sometime around 11:00 a.m. on August 15, Hatanaka placed a pistol to his forehead and shot himself. Shiizaki stabbed himself with a dagger and then shot himself. There was a death poem in Hatanaka's pocket. It read, "I have nothing to regret now that the dark clouds have disappeared from the reign of the emperor."

General Tanaka was regarded as the hero of the August 15 incident and credited with bringing an end to the attempted coup d'état singlehandedly. Tanaka did not embrace being a hero as he felt responsible for the damage Tokyo had sustained from the Allied bombings. Since March 19, he had attempted to resign three times, after he failed to prevent damage to the Meiji Shrine, the Imperial Palace, and other important sites, but his resignation requests were all refused. When the war was concluded, Tanaka ordered his subordinates to destroy the unit colors. He also ordered them not to commit suicide, as he intended to commit suicide himself on behalf of all his men. Nine days after the siege of the palace, General Tanaka ended his life.

After order was restored at the Imperial Palace, the emperor's recorded speech was broadcast to the nation on August 15 at noon Japanese standard time. The speech was translated into English by Tadaichi Hirakawa and broadcast overseas at the same time. In the United States, the Federal Communications Commission recorded the broadcast and its entire text was published in *The New York Times*.

*After pondering deeply the general trends of the world and the actual conditions obtaining in Our Empire today, We have decided to effect a settlement of the present situation by resorting to an extraordinary measure.*

*We have ordered Our Government to communicate to the Governments of the United States, Great Britain, China and the Soviet Union that Our Empire accepts the provisions of their Joint Declaration.*

*To strive for the common prosperity and happiness of all nations as well as the security and well-being of Our subjects is the solemn obligation which has been handed down by Our Imperial Ancestors and which lies close to Our heart.*

*Indeed, We declared war on America and Britain out of Our sincere desire to ensure Japan's self-preservation and the stabilization of East Asia, it being far from Our thought either to infringe upon the sovereignty of other nations or to embark upon territorial aggrandizement.*

*But now the war has lasted for nearly four years. Despite the best that has been done by everyone – the gallant fighting of the military and naval forces, the diligence and assiduity of Our servants of the State, and the devoted service of Our one hundred million people – the war situation has developed not necessarily to Japan's advantage, while the general trends of the world have all turned against her interest.*

*Moreover, the enemy has begun to employ a new and most cruel bomb, the power of which to do damage is, indeed, incalculable, taking the toll of many innocent lives. Should we continue to fight, not only would it result in an ultimate collapse and obliteration of the Japanese nation, but also it would lead to the total extinction of human civilization.*

*Such being the case, how are We to save the millions of Our subjects, or to atone Ourselves before the hallowed spirits of Our Imperial Ancestors? This is the reason why We have ordered the acceptance of the provisions of the Joint Declaration of the Powers....*

*The hardships and sufferings to which Our nation is to be subjected hereafter will be certainly great. We are keenly aware of the inmost feelings of all of you, Our subjects. However, it is according to the dictates of time and fate that We have resolved to pave the way for a grand peace for all the generations to come by enduring the unendurable and suffering what is insufferable.*

The emperor never spoke explicitly about surrender or defeat but simply remarked that the war had not turned in Japan's favor.

Public reaction to the emperor's speech was mixed. After hearing the emperor's words, many Japanese went about their daily activities as best they could. At a military base north of Nagasaki, enraged army officers killed 16 captured American airmen. A large crowd gathered in front of the Imperial Palace in Tokyo and wept. Their cries were interrupted only by the sound of gunshots, as military officers nearby committed suicide.

But if Japan had not surrendered, what would have been next on the United States' agenda? President Truman's announcement of the atomic bombing of Hiroshima had made it clear that the United States would continue with its atomic bombing until Japan surrendered.

What is open to debate, however, is whether the United States actually had a nuclear arsenal to carry out its threat. Official records indicate that a third atomic bomb would be ready in late August, and thereafter one atomic bomb per month would be ready for use throughout 1946.

Activities that took place on Tinian Island further support the theory of a third atomic bomb being dropped on Japan. Tinian Island is situated in the Western Pacific and was the location of the base from which the B-29 bombers took off to drop the uranium-fueled atomic bomb "Little Boy" on Hiroshima and the plutonium-type "Fat Man" on Nagasaki. Prior to the dropping of the nuclear bombs, the bombing units of the 509th Composite Group (509 CG) on Tinian Island had dropped 10,000-pound mock atomic bombs, each containing 5,500 pounds of explosives (known as pumpkin bombs) on 12 targets across Japan before unleashing the real bombs. The dropping of the pumpkin bombs served as a rehearsal, helping air crews to familiarize themselves with the flight routes and confirm their targets. To maximize the impact of the nuclear weapons, the actual targets were omitted from the conventional bombing targets.

The US military had listed the following cities as possible targets on their atomic bomb list: Niigata, Hiroshima, Kokura, Nagasaki, Kyoto, Yokohama and Tokyo. The list was created by a committee of American military generals, army officers and scientists.

On August 14, just one day before the emperor's surrender speech was broadcast, a bombing crew dropped seven pumpkin bombs on Aichi prefecture as part of yet another rehearsal.

The Japanese Instrument of Surrender was signed on the deck of the USS Missouri in Tokyo Bay on September 2, 1945.

The signing ceremony lasted for 23 minutes and was broadcast throughout the world. The first signature was that of Japanese Foreign Minister Mamoru Shigemitsu, followed by the signature of the Chief of the Army General Staff, General Yoshijiro Umezu. Then United States General of the Army, Douglas MacArthur, accepted the surrender of Japan and added his signature as Supreme Commander of the Allied Powers.

The document was also signed by a representative of each of the Allied Powers, including: American Fleet Admiral Chester Nimitz, General Hsu Yung-chang (Republic of China), Admiral Sir Bruce Fraser (United Kingdom), Lieutenant General Kuzma Derevyanko (Soviet Union), General Sir Thomas Blamey (Australia), Colonel Lawrence Moore Cosgrove (Canada), General de Corps d'Armee, Philippe Leclerc de Hauteclocque (France), Lieutenant Admiral C.E.L. Helfrich (Netherlands), and Air Vice-Marshall Leonard M. Isitt (New Zealand).

The Japanese copy of the treaty varied from the Allied copy in that the Allied copy was presented in a leather folder with gold lining bearing both country's seals on the front cover, whereas the Japanese copy was presented in a plain canvas folder without the seals.

With the signing of the official surrender, the emperor was allowed to remain with the stipulation that, "The authority of the emperor and the Japanese government to rule the state shall be subject to the Supreme Commander for the Allied Powers who will take such steps as he deems proper to effectuate these terms of surrender." Although the Japanese emperor's role has historically alternated between a ceremonial role and that of an actual ruler, with the adoption of the Japanese Constitution in 1947, the emperor's status was changed to that of a mere figurehead.

Even after the signing of the Japanese Instrument of Surrender, some isolated soldiers throughout Asia and the Pacific islands refused to surrender for months and even years afterwards, one holding out until the 1970s.

That soldier's name was Hiroo Onoda, a former intelligence officer in the Japanese army. Onoda was sent to the western Philippine island of Lubang in 1944, where he was directed to spy on the American forces. When the Allied forces defeated the Japanese Imperial Army in the Philippines, most of the Japanese troops either withdrew or surrendered. Onoda and a few others, however, evaded capture and hid in the jungle, refusing to believe that World War II had ended despite receiving messages to the contrary.

Although his comrades passed away due to various reasons, Onoda held out for 29 years, subsisting on food he either gathered in the jungle or stole from farmers nearby. It wasn't until March of 1974 when Onoda was finally convinced to come out of hiding. He was 52 years old. When he returned to Japan he was given a hero's welcome, but when he returned to the Philippines in May of 1996, the relatives of those he was accused of killing gathered and demanded compensation. Onoda remained a controversial figure in the Philippines despite being pardoned by the Philippine government. When interviewed by the press, Onoda stated, "Every Japanese soldier was prepared for death, but as an intelligence officer I was ordered to conduct guerrilla warfare and not to die. I had to follow my orders as I was a soldier."

# KEY DATES DURING THE ALLIED
# OCCUPATION OF JAPAN

| 1945 | |
|---|---|
| August 28 | 150 US personnel arrive at Atsugi in Kanagawa prefecture. |
| August 28 | The RAA (Recreation and Amusement Association) created. |
| August 30 | General Douglas MacArthur arrives in Tokyo. |
| September 2 | Japan signs the Japanese Instrument of Surrender. |
| September 6 | President Truman approves the US Initial Post-Surrender Policy for Japan. |
| September 10 | The Supreme Commander for the Allied Powers (SCAP) issues press and pre-censorship codes outlawing the publication of all reports and statistics relating to news of criminal activities, such as rape, and other issues "inimical to the objectives of the Occupation." |
| September 27 | General MacArthur meets with Emperor Hirohito. |
| October 4 | The Removal of Restrictions on Political, Civil, and Religious Liberties directive issued, repealing the Peace Preservation Law, the Thought Control Law, and releasing all political prisoners. |

| | |
|---|---|
| November 6 | SCAP issues a directive for the elimination of undemocratic motion pictures. |
| December 15 | Shinto Directive issued, abolishing Shinto as a state religion and prohibiting some of its teachings and rites. |
| December 22 | Trade Union Law passed, allowing workers to organize, strike and bargain collectively. |
| December 31 | SCAP issues a directive to suspend all courses in Japanese history, geography, and morals. |
| **1946** | |
| January 1 | Emperor Hirohito signs the *Ningen-Sengen (The Humanity Declaration)* renouncing his divinity. |
| February 21 | The British Commonwealth Occupation Force, comprised of Australian, British, Indian, and New Zealand personnel deployed to Japan to assist with supervising demilitarization. |
| March 17 | SCAP issues a directive for the confiscation of propaganda, books, and publications. On March 20 they introduced a list of forbidden books. |
| March 27 | The RAA is shut down. |
| April 10 | First general election held. |
| April 26 | The International Military Tribunal for the Far East is convened. |
| October 11 | Land Reform Law passed. |

| 1947 | |
|---|---|
| April 7 | The Labor Standards Act is enacted to govern working conditions in Japan. |
| May 3 | The Constitution of Japan is enacted. |
| 1949 | |
| January 6 | SCAP issues a directive authorizing the Japanese to display and use the national flag without restrictions. |
| May 11 | SCAP issues a directive to allow security exchanges to be opened in Tokyo, Osaka, and Nagoya. |
| July 29 | General Macarthur decrees a drastic reduction of personnel in the US Military Government, signifying a return to Japanese autonomy. |
| 1950 | |
| June 25 | Beginning of the Korean War. |
| 1951 | |
| April 11 | General MacArthur replaced by Lieutenant General Ridgway. |
| April 16 | General MacArthur departs Japan. |
| April 18 | Allied trials of Japanese war criminals come to an end. |
| September 8 | The San Francisco Peace Treaty is signed marking the end of the Allied occupation. |
| 1952 | |
| April 28 | Japan's sovereignty fully restored. |

# THE ALLIED OCCUPATION OF JAPAN

When Emperor Hirohito announced Japan's unconditional surrender on the radio on August 15, 1945, it was his first radio broadcast and the first time the majority of Japanese citizens actually heard his voice. This date became known as V-J Day or Victory over Japan Day in America. The same name was given to September 2, 1945, when the Japanese officially signed the surrender document aboard the battleship USS Missouri. In Japan, however, August 15 was known as *Shusen Kinenbi* (Memorial Day for the End of the War). This name was officially changed in 1982 by an ordinance adopted by the Japanese government, and today August 15 is known as *Senbotsusha o Tsuitoshi Heiwa o Kinensuru Hi* (Day For Mourning of War Dead and Praying for Peace).

On August 28, 150 United States personnel arrived at Atsugi City in Kanagawa prefecture. The Atsugi Kaigun Hikojo (the Naval Air Facility Atsugi) is located just 7.4 km (4.6 miles) east-northeast of the city, and it is the largest United States naval air base in the Pacific Ocean today. The United States shares the base with the Japan Maritime Self-Defense Force.

The base was originally constructed in 1938 by the Imperial Japanese Navy and was home to the Japanese 302 Naval Aviation Corps, one of Japan's most formidable fighter squadrons during World War II. It is documented that aircraft based at Atsugi Kaigun Hikojo managed to shoot down over 300 American bombers during the fire bombings of 1945. Following Japan's surrender, many of the Japanese pilots stationed at the base refused to follow the emperor's orders to lay down their arms. Instead, they took to the skies and dropped countless leaflets over the cities of Tokyo and Yokohama, urging locals to resist the American forces. Eventually, these pilots gave up and abandoned Atsugi.

General Douglas MacArthur, appointed as the Supreme Commander of the Allied Forces, arrived in Tokyo on August 30. Although Great Britain, the Soviet Union, and the Republic of China had an advisory role as part of the Allied Council, MacArthur had the final authority to make all decisions. Shortly after his arrival, several laws were put into place. Allied personnel were forbidden to assault the Japanese people or to eat their scarce food. Japanese people were forbidden to fly the *Hinomaru*, or Rising Sun flag, until 1948, when the restriction was partially lifted. It was fully lifted a year later.

Despite these laws, the US troops committed countless rapes throughout Japan, many of which went unreported.

Following the Battle of Okinawa, thousands of rapes occurred on the Ryukyu Islands. There were 76 cases of rape or rape-murder reported in Okinawa alone during the first five years of occupation.

But perhaps the most disturbing of these cases took place ten years into the United States occupation of Okinawa. The case, referred to as the Yumiko Nagayama Incident, involved the rape and murder of a six-year-old child by a 31-year-old American soldier named Isaac J. Hurt. Sergeant Hurt was a member of B Battalion, 32nd Artillery Division and stationed in Okinawa. The little girl was reported missing on September 3, 1955 and her mutilated body was discovered in a garbage dump at Kadena Air Base the next day.

Sergeant Hurt was brought up on rape and murder charges by a United States court-martial, convicted, and sentenced to death. However, his case was later appealed. He was returned to the United States and was set free. At the time, he was the second

United States serviceman convicted of rape in Okinawa in less than one month.

The sexual crimes committed in Okinawa prompted the Japanese authorities to set up a system of prostitution facilities known as the Recreation and Amusement Association (RAA) to protect the Japanese women living on the mainland. The organization was created on August 28 and was initially referred to as the "Special Comfort Facilities Association."

By the end of 1945, more than 350,000 United States personnel were stationed throughout Japan. The Japanese strategy was to utilize "experienced women" to protect the average women and girls from harm. They established 34 facilities, 16 of which were actually used for prostitution. At its peak, the RAA had 20,000 prostitutes working for the organization.

But where did the RAA get 20,000 "experienced women?" It was a well-known fact that the Japanese government had cracked down on prostitution in Tokyo, prompting many women in the trade to flee the city. Also, the famous Yoshiwara red light district only had 2,000 prostitutes prior to the war and that number dwindled down to only a few dozen by the war's end.

Therefore, the RAA recruited widely from the general population, using carefully worded advertisements posted in front of their offices and in newspapers. These ads emphasized generous work conditions, which included free accommodation, meals, and clothes, and avoided providing the actual details concerning the nature of the work. Most women left upon learning of the deception, but some stayed.

Many of those that did stay did so due to the desperate financial situation of their families. There were widespread poverty and food shortages at the time. Many of the women were urged by their parents to become prostitutes or possessed a willingness to sacrifice themselves to help their families. The RAA also took advantage of the large number of orphaned and widowed young women.

In addition to the prostitutes, the RAA also recruited a large number of "dancers" who were paid to dance with soldiers. However, over time, the distinction between "dancer" and "prostitute" became blurred.

Faced with the unprecedented rise in venereal disease among the American soldiers, MacArthur closed down the prostitution facilities on March 27, 1946, after which time the incidence of rape increased significantly. When the RAA was in existence, it was estimated that the number of rapes and assaults on Japanese women averaged 40 incidences per day. After the closure of the facilities, that number increased to an average of 330 incidences per day. The sexual and violent crimes were most prevalent in naval ports, such as Yokohama and Yokosuka. Two weeks into the occupation, the Occupation Administration began censoring all media, including any mention of rape or other sensitive social issues. However, this did not completely prevent the local newspapers from leaking information from time to time. One example was the local newspaper, Daily Ise Shimbun, which was suspended for twenty-four hours on December 27, 1945, for violating the Allied Press Code.

The closing of the RAA also saw the rise of what became known as "pan-pan girls." The term was a derogatory one and used to describe prostitutes who walked the streets. Many women who worked for the RAA suddenly found themselves out of work when the organization closed its doors. Consequently, they took to the streets and became private and illegal prostitutes. The pan-pan girls dressed in Western attire and solicited around bars, public transport stations, and on the street. They were often seen walking down the street holding on to the arms of tall, uniformed American GIs. These women soon became the symbols of the Allied Occupation of Japan.

On September 6, President Harry S. Truman approved the United States Initial Post-Surrender Policy for Japan. It was drafted by the State-War-Navy Coordinating Committee and set two main objectives for the occupation:

(1) To insure that Japan will not again become a menace to the United States or to the peace and security of the world.

(2) To bring about the eventual establishment of a peaceful and responsible government which will respect the rights of other states and will support the objectives of the United States as reflected in the ideals and principles of the Charter of the United Nations.

A vast majority of Japanese citizens were virtually starving after the collapse of their government and the destruction of their major cities. Rather than adhering to the United States Initial Post-Surrender Policy for Japan, General MacArthur's first act as Supreme Commander was to set up a food distribution network. While the United States sent billions of dollars to Japan in food aid, this cost was small in comparison to the occupation costs that were imposed on the struggling Japanese administration.

Once the food distribution network was in place, the general met with Emperor Hirohito. The meeting took place on September 27.

While several Allied political and military leaders pushed to have the emperor tried as a war criminal, MacArthur argued against it stating that such a move would be devastatingly unpopular with the Japanese people, who revered their sovereign. Even though members of the Imperial Family urged the emperor's abdication, such as Prince Takahito Mikasa, the fourth and youngest son of Emperor Taisho and Empress Teimei, and Prince Naruhiko Higashikuni, an uncle-in-law of Emperor Hirohito, the General rejected it.

General MacArthur and Emperor Hirohito met several times during MacArthur's tenure as Supreme Commander for the Allied Powers. All of the meetings were highly choreographed affairs and followed set agendas.

General MacArthur later urged Emperor Hirohito to renounce his divine status. He obliged on January 1, 1946 by signing a document known as *Ningen-Sengen* (The Humanity Declaration). The document included the following passage:

*The ties between Us and Our people have always stood upon mutual trust and affection. They do not depend upon mere legends and myths. They are not predicated on the false conception that the Emperor is divine, and that the Japanese people are superior to other races and fated to rule the world.*

Ironically, although Emperor Hirohito renounced his divine status, he never actually denied being a direct descendant of goddess Amaterasu.

On October 4, 1945 General MacArthur issued the Removal of Restrictions on Political, Civil, and Religious Liberties, also known as the (SCAPIN-93) directive. The directive aimed to dismantle the oppressive policies of the pre-1945 Japanese government and allow citizens the freedom to criticize the Emperor of Japan. Hence, the Peace Preservation Law and the Thought Control Law (the Ideological Prisoner Custody and Surveillance Laws) were repealed as a result. The directive also contributed to the release of 3,000 political prisoners.

The next stage of the occupation was the disarmament of Japan. Japan's postwar constitution included a peace clause (Article 9), which banned Japan from maintaining any military forces. Although the clause was put in place by the Japanese government and was intended to prevent the country from ever becoming an aggressive military power, the United States soon began to pressure Japan to rebuild its army in an effort to safeguard the country against communism.

Following the 1917 communist revolution in Russia, there were calls by Western leaders to isolate the Bolshevik government, which seemed intent on promoting worldwide revolution. After Germany invaded the Union of Soviet Socialist Republics during World War II, the United States and the Soviet Union found themselves allied in their opposition to Germany. When the war concluded and the need to unite to defeat Germany and Japan had disappeared, the differences between the capitalist West and communist East came to the forefront once again. The United States was becoming increasingly alarmed by the spread of communism in Europe. President Harry S. Truman told Congress in March of 1947 that America could no longer stand back and allow communism to spread any further. This policy of containment became known as the Truman Doctrine. The Truman Doctrine made it possible for America to send military advisors, support personnel, and money to foreign countries to help combat the spread of communism.

In the post-war world, communist systems spread throughout a number of countries and China was not exempt. On October 1, 1949, Mao Zedong proclaimed the People's Republic of China, marking the beginning of the Communist Era.

This led the United States government to formulate the domino theory, which governed much of America's foreign policy beginning in the early 1950s. The theory stated that a communist victory in one nation would quickly lead to a chain reaction of communist takeovers in neighboring states.

Consequently, Japan created the National Police Reserve, and in 1954 the Japan Self-Defense Forces were founded. In recent times, Prime Ministers Junichiro Koizumi and Shinzo Abe have tried unsuccessfully to repeal the peace clause. Although the peace clause still remains in place, Japan today maintains the eighth largest military budget in the world.

In late 1947, the Occupation Administration shifted their focus to internal political stability and economic growth. As a result, many of the financial coalitions known as the *zaibatsu* were abolished.

The zaibatsu were industrial and financial business conglomerates who exercised significant control of the Japanese economy from the Meiji period through the end of World War II. During the 1920s and 1930s, when a majority of the world was in the grip of economic depression, the zaibatsu prospered through military procurement, speculating in currency, and maintaining low labor costs. The "Big Four" or *yondai zaibatsu* consisted of Sumitomo, Mitsui, Mitsubishi and Yasuda. Sumitomo and Mitsui, in particular, date back to the Edo period. During the Meiji and Showa periods, the Japanese government relied on the zaibatsu for tax collection, military procurement, and foreign trade.

Following the Russo-Japanese War, a second-tier zaibatsu emerged and included the Okura, Furukawa, and Nakajima groups.

During the Allied occupation, the zaibatsu with their restrictive business practices were considered inefficient and anti-democratic. As a result, 16 were targeted for complete dissolution and 26 were targeted for reorganization. The controlling families' assets were seized, their holding companies eliminated, and interlocking directorships were outlawed. However, complete dissolution of the zaibatsu was never achieved.

On October 11, 1946, Japan passed the Land Reform Law. Between 1947 and 1949, approximately 23,000 km2 (5,800,000 acres) of land were purchased from the landlords under the government's reform program and resold at extremely low prices to the farmers. By 1950, three million farmers became land owners, dismantling a power structure long dominated by the landlords.

Next, the focus shifted to the state religion. The occupation authorities deemed Shinto's teachings and rites to be militaristic or ultra-nationalistic. Therefore, on December 15, 1945, the Shinto Directive was issued, abolishing Shinto as the state religion.

Although Shinto is no longer a state religion, many Japanese still regard Shinto as the national/ethnic religion, and it is practiced by nearly 80% of the population. To date, there are 81,000 Shinto shrines and 85,000 priests throughout Japan.

Post-war Shinto is very different from the pre-1946 version. It has been cleansed of the political, nationalistic and militaristic elements that were included in state Shinto.

But even with the cleansing, controversy still remains to this day regarding one of its most famous shrines, the Imperial Shrine of Yasukuni *(Yasukuni Jinja)*, located in the Chiyoda Ward of Tokyo. It was founded by the Meiji Emperor and commemorates all who have fallen in the service of the Empire of Japan. Over the years, the list has been expanded to include the names, birthdates, and places of death of nearly 2.5 million people and animals. Among those listed are 1,068 people who are considered to be war criminals, and 14 of the 1,068 are considered to be A-Class, hence the controversy. Active Japanese diplomats who have visited the shrine have been scorned by the global media.

According to the military tribunals, an A-Class war criminal is someone who is involved in crimes against peace, such as plotting and waging war. Those who were involved in more unusual war crimes, such as executing helpless prisoners, were classified as a B-Class and those that were involved with crimes against humanity, such as genocide, were classified as C-Class.

Various military tribunals were taking place at the same time as the reforms. Japan's war criminals were tried and sentenced to death or imprisonment. However, there were many suspects who managed to escape prosecution for their war crimes in one way or another.

One such person was Masanobu Tsuji, a Japanese army officer and politician who was said to be deeply involved in Japanese atrocities throughout the war. He was an important tactical planner and among the most aggressive and influential Japanese militarists. He was also a vehement advocate of war with the United States. Tsuji managed to evade prosecution for war crimes by hiding in Thailand. When he returned to Japan in 1949, he was elected to the Diet, Japan's bicameral legislature. He traveled to

Laos in 1961, and his whereabouts have been unknown since then.

Another person who narrowly escaped prosecution was Nobusuke Kishi. He was a Japanese politician and the 56th and 57th Prime Minister of Japan. He is the maternal grandfather of Japan's current Prime Minister, Shinzo Abe. In October of 1941, Kishi was appointed as the Munitions Minister. In this role, he was involved in forcing Koreans and Chinese to work as slaves in Japan's factories and mines during the war. Under Kishi, 670,000 Koreans and 41,862 Chinese were forced to work as slave laborers in what was deemed to be the most degrading conditions in Japan. The majority did not survive the experience. After the war, Kishi was held at the Sugamo Prison as an A-Class war crimes suspect. Fortunately for Kishi, a group of influential Americans who had formed the American Council on Japan came to his aid and lobbied the American government to release him, as they considered Kishi to be the best man to lead a post-war Japan in a pro-American direction. Kishi was released in 1948 and was never indicted or tried.

There were others, like Yoshio Kodama, a prominent figure in the organized crime world who helped to move supplies for the Japanese war effort out of continental Asia and into Japan, and Ryoichi Sasakawa, a Japanese businessman, politician, and philanthropist who also escaped prosecution, although both were imprisoned in the Sugamo Prison. Emperor Hirohito and all the members of the Imperial Family were granted immunity by General MacArthur.

On April 10, 1946, an election was held in which Japan's first modern prime minister, Shigeru Yoshida, was elected. A new Constitution was ratified by the Japanese Diet in 1947. It transferred sovereignty from the emperor to the people, making the sovereign's role purely symbolic. The Constitution also empowered women, guaranteed fundamental human rights, strengthened the powers of Parliament and the Cabinet, and decentralized the police and local governments.

The nisei who volunteered or were drafted to serve in the United States military performed duties as translators, interpreters, and investigators for the International Military Tribunal, which tried and sentenced Japanese war criminals. There were over 5,000 Japanese Americans who served in the occupation of Japan.

The San Francisco Peace Treaty was signed on September 8, 1951, ending the Allied occupation of Japan. In April of 1952, Japan's sovereignty was restored although the U.S. still maintains bases in and around Tokyo, Okinawa, Kanagawa, and Nagasaki.

Japan emerged from the Allied occupation a free, peaceful, and democratic society, albeit with various residual issues. As the GIs began to withdraw from the country the United States had occupied for seven years, some took with them more than just memories. Others left behind an often untold legacy.

Some of the returning soldiers brought home Japanese brides. Thousands of young Japanese women married American soldiers despite their own families' shock and disapproval. Americans were seen as the enemy by the Japanese, but then again, there was incredible hatred and fear on both sides following the war.

A majority of these Japanese war brides were well educated and came from wealthy families, and they could not see a future in war-torn Japan. Major cities like Tokyo lay in ruins, and people were struggling for food and shelter. These women did not know much about the men they were marrying but accepted the soldiers' marriage requests as a means of survival and sought to make a better life for themselves in the United States.

Many were disappointed when they arrived in the United States; however, as anti-Japanese sentiment ran high and they faced discrimination from both Americans and the Japanese American community. The Japanese Americans had endured such horrendous experiences in the American internment camps that they wanted nothing to do with the Japanese women from Japan.

When World War II concluded, Japanese migrants were excluded from entering the United States. Although the War Brides Act of 1945 permitted American GIs who married abroad to bring their wives home, it wasn't until the enactment of the Immigration Act (McCarran-Walter Act) of 1952 that the Japanese were once again permitted to come to the United States.

There were 30,000 to 35,000 Japanese women who migrated to the United States during the 1950s. Upon arrival, some attended Japanese bride schools at military bases to learn how to do things the American way, but many were totally unprepared for their new role.

Some were given American names, and they were not permitted to wear the beautiful kimonos they had brought with them from Japan. The differences in American lifestyle contradicted their Japanese upbringing, and they were horrified.

Most of these women were ashamed to tell their relatives about the challenges they faced in their new world and instead wrote glowing letters to their families in Japan.

The GI husbands were unprepared as well. More often than not, they expected a wife that was more submissive than an American woman and at the same time expected that she would cook American meals and raise children with American values.

Often these interracial marriages ended in divorce, not because of the differences between the American and Japanese cultures but because of the incompatibility of the couples themselves.

The end of the occupation also resulted in thousands of mixed-race children left behind by GI fathers who either never knew of their existence or refused to acknowledge them. Despite the passage of the McCarran-Walter Act, immigration quotas based on national origin remained in place in the United States until 1965 and directly affected the mixed-race children born during the occupation. Deserted wives and children were denied automatic right of entry to the United Stated unless the husbands and fathers acknowledged them.

Some of the *konketsuji* (mixed-blood children) were abandoned in orphanages while others were adopted by their Japanese mother's family members. In either case, the children indisputably suffered from discrimination.

These children were Japanese in essentially every regard, including language, mindset, and cultural orientation. The only discerning characteristic was their appearance. Japan has had a long history of both tolerance and discrimination toward foreigners and mixed-race children.

The first foreigners arrived in Japan in 1543; they were three shipwrecked Portuguese traders. In 1549, Father Francis Xavier, a Jesuit missionary arrived seeking to spread Christianity to a polytheistic society. Soon, foreign merchant ships began to visit the port city of Nagasaki regularly. Some of the merchants remained in Japan and formed unions with the daughters of prominent samurai and wealthy Japanese merchants. The mixed-race children resulting from these unions were tolerated by ordinary Japanese citizens, but Japan's rulers soon became alarmed by the spread of foreign blood in their country. In 1635, the Tokugawa enacted the Sakoku Edict, which began Japan's two hundred year seclusion and was intended to eliminate foreign influence. In 1636, another edict was enacted calling for the deportation of the wives and children of the foreign merchants. Soon after the enactment, four ships set sail from Nagasaki carrying 287 people who were warned not to return under penalty of death. Only a small handful of Dutch people were allowed to remain, and they were confined to an island off of Nagasaki called Dejima. These measures were said to be necessary to preserve the country's traditions and territorial integrity.

Even after Japan opened her ports to foreigners following the collapse of the Tokugawa Shogunate, the Japanese view toward mixed-race children was varied and intolerance coexisted with pragmatism.

When the prevailing views of the time are combined with the post-war shortages in Japan and the already existing population of war orphans who had resulted from the staggering number of servicemen and civilians killed during World War II, it becomes clear as to why the konketsuji were discriminated against.

There were an estimated 2,000 to 6,500 orphans residing in Hiroshima alone after the war. These children had lost their family members after the atomic bomb was dropped on their city. Some lived in the various war casualty children's homes, but many more ended up living on the street, doing what they could to survive.

The babies born to American servicemen and Japanese women were estimated to number 5,000 to 10,000 by 1952. The occupation forces also consisted of Australian, British, Indian and New Zealand personnel (the British Commonwealth Occupation Force (BCOF)) who also fathered children with Japanese women.

While the motivation for survival and self-preservation existed during the post-war years, there were an ambitious few who sought to help the konketsuji. Perhaps the most famous was a Japanese social worker named Miki Sawada.

Miki Sawada was born in Oiso, a town located in Kanagawa prefecture. She was the daughter of Baron Hisaya Iwasaki and the granddaughter of Yataro Iwasaki, the founder of the Mitsubishi zaibatsu. She had the privilege of traveling extensively as the wife of Renzo Sawada, the former Japanese vice-minister of foreign affairs and ambassador to the United Nations. During her travels she volunteered at an orphanage in England, and upon returning home she was horrified by the number of homeless and abandoned children. She established the Elizabeth Saunders Home in Oiso in 1948, on the land which once housed her family's residence. The Japanese government had confiscated the home in lieu of property tax payment during World War II. Sawada managed to buy it back for ¥4 million, which she raised in part by selling her personal property. In time, Sawada became known as the mother of 2,000 American Japanese mixed-race orphans.

# THE SUN WILL RISE AGAIN: JAPAN STRUGGLES TO REBUILD

After decades of being brainwashed into believing that Japan possessed a superior military force, and that Japan's victory in a war would most certainly be inevitable, the Japanese people were profoundly shocked to hear Emperor Hirohito's broadcast in which he surrendered to the Allies.

However, for the many Japanese who were facing starvation and homelessness, concerns about defeat were only secondary.

Japan was in a state of chaos following the end of World War II. Millions of people dwelling in the country's urban centers found themselves displaced as a result of the Allied air raids and fire bombings. Poor harvests, the cessation of food imports from occupied territories, and the demands of war created food shortages.

In the months following October 1945, over 5.1 million Japanese living in other parts of Asia had to be repatriated. These individuals were primarily from Japan's former colonies of Korea, Manchuria, Taiwan, and the Pacific islands. Although over a million former colonial subjects were deported from Japan during the same time period, the repatriation put a strain on Japan's already scarce resources. Drug and alcohol abuse soared.

Methamphetamine, known as *Hiropon* in Japan, was distributed by the military to fighter pilots during World War II to help them stay awake and alert. Methamphetamine was first synthesized in 1893 by a Japanese chemist named Nagai Nagayoshi.

The Japanese military was not alone in administering the drug to its soldiers. Germany provided the drug to its entire armed forces under the brand name Pervitin during World War II.

In post-war Japan, the large military stockpiles of methamphetamine found their way into the black market and a Hiropon epidemic emerged. One of the short-term side effects of Hiropon usage is decreased appetite, which might have been seen as beneficial when there were vast food shortages all over Japan. Fortunately, by the mid-1950s, and the passage of stricter laws, Hiropon abuse was almost totally eradicated.

Methamphetamine was not the only drug Japan relied on during the war. A 21-page document titled *Outline of Hóng Jì Shàn Tang* was discovered in an archive at the National Diet Library of Tokyo, details the operations of a Japanese narcotics firm in wartime occupied China. The firm sold enough opium to nearly equal the annual budget of Tokyo's government in occupied Nanking. The annual budget of the Nanking government in 1941 was 370 million yuan. The document reveals that Hóng Jì Shàn Tang sold opium worth 300 million yuan in the same year. What is important to note is that Japan's opium trade in China was considered to be an essential financial resource for the Imperial Japanese Army and Japan's governments in occupied territories.

Hóng Jì Shàn Tang was technically a private company headed by a man named Hajime Satomi. Profits from the opium trade bankrolled the Imperial army's unofficial spying activities that were not covered by the official military budget. Later, revenue from the opium monopoly became a major financial source for the governments of Inner Mongolia, Nanking, and Manchuria.

Hajime Satomi was arrested as a suspected Class-A war criminal by the Allied powers, but for reasons that have not been determined he was never indicted. He was later released and died in 1965 of cardiac failure at the age of 69. He is buried in an obscure tomb located at Soneiji Temple in Ichikawa, Chiba prefecture. The inscription on his tombstone was written by former Prime Minister Nobusuke Kishi, a grandfather of Prime Minister Shinzo Abe. When questioned, Kishi claimed that he became acquainted with Satomi after the war and wrote the inscription on his tombstone at the request of an acquaintance.

But the truth is that Kishi was a senior government official in the Japanese-occupied state of Manchukuo in Manchuria between 1936 and 1939, when both he and General Hideki Tojo reportedly established close relations with Satomi. It has been alleged that many politicians and military officers at that time, including Kishi and Tojo, approached Satomi for political funds resulting from the opium trade. Kishi met General Tojo when the latter headed the Japanese military police units in Manchukuo. When Tojo later became the Prime Minister shortly before the Pearl Harbor attack in December 1941, he appointed Kishi as his wartime industry minister.

In a written statement submitted to the postwar Nanking trial of Chinese leaders accused of collaborating with Japan, Mei Siping (梅思平), a Kuomintang politician of the Republic of China revealed that the majority of the profits from drug sales in Shanghai and other Chinese cities were funneled directly to Tokyo. During the time of the Tojo Cabinet, the money was allotted as secret funds for the Cabinet, which used it to subsidize members of the Diet. His statement was further corroborated by Major General Ryukichi Tanaka during the 1946 pretrial interrogation by prosecutors for the International Military Tribunal for the Far East. Tanaka stated that Tojo received great sums of money from Satomi's secret opium funds, and that Lieutenant General Kiyonobu Shiozawa, Tojo's most favored protégé, was also a close friend of Satomi. Tanaka further added that Shiozawa traveled from Tokyo to Beijing approximately every two months and brought back large sums of money for Tojo. Shiozawa headed the Beijing office of the China Affairs Board, a Japanese wartime government body. When called as a witness in the Tokyo tribunal, Satomi testified that he had handed over all the profits of his opium business to the China Affairs Board and the Imperial Army.

The military stockpiles of methamphetamine were not the only goods found on the Japanese black market in post-war Japan. Inflation was widespread and people turned to the black market for even the most basic items necessary to live. The newspapers in Tokyo reported that since the war had ended, approximately 1,400 people had starved to death in Japan's major cities.

On November 17, 1945, the first major food riot took place in Hokkaido. Thousands of men and women broke into a flour mill, looted carts carrying grains, and made off with whatever they were able to seize. The following day, approximately 1,300 rioters broke into stores and took what they could carry. In one case, the looters left money behind to pay for the items they had taken.

On November 23, 1945, approximately 200 Japanese citizens broke into an American army warehouse in Sendai and took food and other items before being dispersed by American military police.

On May 19, 1946, 250,000 demonstrators converged on Tokyo. A Communist leader, Kyuchi Tokuda, was among them and was inciting the crowd. He asked them, "We are starving, what about him? "(referring to the emperor).

The black markets were very lucrative, and often controlled by rival gangs. Fights for control of the markets were inevitable.

One particular incident was known as the *Shibuya jiken* (the Shibuya Incident). It took place in June of 1946 and involved the Taiwanese gang (Taiwan was formerly called Formosa and was a province of Japan from 1895 to 1945) and the Japanese Yakuza group, Matsuba-kai.

Fighting took place outside the Shibuya police station where over a thousand Matsuba members fought hundreds of Taiwanese gang members with clubs, metal pipes, and small firearms. Seven Taiwanese were killed and thirty-four were wounded. One Japanese policeman was killed and another injured. The public was outraged and blamed the non-Japanese Asians and the incompetence of the Japanese police for the incident.

Over forty Taiwanese were arrested in connection with the Shibuya jiken, but their cases were quickly taken up by the Chinese component of the Allied command in Tokyo. The men were given a public trial, which resulted in thirty-five convictions. After being convicted, these people faced either sentences of hard labor or deportation.

As if the food shortages and homelessness were not enough for the Japanese to bear, in January 1946 a smallpox epidemic broke out in Japan; the highest incidences of disease were reported in Hokkaido, Kyoto, and Osaka. The epidemic reached its peak in March when 1,405 new patients were diagnosed. In April a typhus epidemic struck, and the highest rates of infection were reported in Tokyo and Kanagawa. There were 32,366 cases of typhus documented, which resulted in 3,351 deaths.

During the post-war years, a term was coined in Japan to describe the rampant exhaustion, declining morale, and despair faced by the general population. That term was *kyodatsujoutai* (kyodatsu condition). There was also a phrase, *shikata ga nai* (it cannot be helped), that was commonly used by both the Japanese and American press to express the Japanese public's resignation to the harsh conditions that existed during the occupation.

These were the conditions which returning Japanese servicemen had to endure. Many had already been exposed to humiliating circumstances, having been sent home in war-damaged carriers and aged, rusting liberty ships  they were packed into like sardines. The majority of the servicemen were suffering from malnutrition and dysentery. When they arrived in Japan, they removed the badges and insignia from their uniforms so they could not be distinguished from civilians easily. The servicemen were also subjected to medical examinations and deloused with DDT before being given a one-way train ticket to their final destination. Like their Allied counterparts, they had difficulty adjusting to civilian life and sought to escape from their horrific memories and find a substitute for the wartime camaraderie they had once enjoyed. This led to the emergence of motorcycle gangs known as *Kaminari Zoku*.

They were called Kaminari Zoku (Thunder Tribe) due to the thunderous roar of their motorcycle engines when they rode through the streets in groups. The violent motorcycle sub-culture known as *Bosozoku* (Reckless Speeding Tribe) that came into existence in the 1970s evolved from the Kaminari Zoku. The main difference between the Kaminari Zoku and the Bosozoku was that the former was born out of a time of severe hardship and deprivation in Japan, while the later came into existence during a time of national prosperity.

The Kaminari Zoku often included surviving kamikaze pilots that hailed from poor families. Naturally, these families were more severely impacted by the post-war shortages. The returning veterans used their motorcycle gang activities to express anger and hostility not only toward the occupation forces but also toward mainstream Japanese society.

Moving into the 1950s, Japan saw the emergence of the *kasutori* culture. Named after the inferior form of homemade *shochu* (alcohol) which circulated after the war, it placed emphasis on escapism, entertainment, and decadence and was a response to the scarcity prominent during the post-war years. Members of this culture consisted predominantly of artists and writers who were known to imbibe in the kasutori sold in the black market by the Kaminari Zoku members.

The Kaminari Zoku eventually faded away in the late 1960s and early 1970s. Some former members found a niche for themselves in mainstream Japanese society while others moved on to become low ranking members of the local *Yakuza* (crime syndicate) gangs.

But not everyone reacted in the same manner to the hardships of the post-war period. While some people succumbed to the difficulties, many others were more resilient. As the country regained its footing, they too were able to recover.

As Japan shifted from being a nation at war to both a democracy and a demilitarized country, other changes also took place. These changes included respect for human rights, gender equality, freedom of speech, and perhaps most importantly, the empowerment of women.

Prior to the post-war years, many Japanese women were constrained by feudalistic and chauvinistic traditions. This changed after the war as Japanese women were allowed to assume new roles in society in addition to being wives and mothers.

During the general election of 1946, over one-third of the votes were cast by women. This high female voter turnout led to the election of 39 female candidates and increased the presence of women in politics.

The post-war Japanese entertainment industry also played a large part in redefining women's roles and behaviors. The industry expunged the older traditional women's roles and created a new, idealized modern female persona.

The most popular female star during the early post-war period was none other than Misora Hibari (1937–89), who became an icon of proper Japanese femininity. She made her debut on stage in 1945 at a Yokohama concert hall. Later, she became a teenage film star, and upon her death in 1989 she was recognized as the most famous *Enka* performer (a popular Japanese music genre consisting of sentimental ballads) to have ever lived.

Misora Hibari was born Kazue Kato in Yokohama, Japan. Her father was a fishmonger, and her mother was a traditional Japanese housewife. She showed promise as a singer at an early age, which prompted her father to  use the family's savings to help launch her musical career.

A year after her debut, Hibari appeared on an NHK broadcast and shortly afterwards started performing in notable concert halls and playing to sold-out crowds. She recorded her first record in 1949 at the age of twelve and starred in her first film the same year. In her lifetime she acted in 160 films and recorded 1,200 songs. In her role as a street orphan in the film *Tokyo Kid* (1950), she became a symbol of both the hardship and the national optimism of post-war Japan.

Hibari was awarded a Medal of Honor for her contributions to music and for improving the welfare of the public. She was the first woman to receive the People's Honor Award, which was conferred posthumously for giving the public hope and encouragement after World War II.

The post-war years also had a great impact on relationships between Japanese men and women. The "modern girl" phenomenon of the 1920s and early 1930s had been characterized by greater sexual freedom; but despite this, sex was usually not perceived as a source of pleasure for Japanese women. As a result, Westerners were thought to be promiscuous and sexually deviant. The sexual liberation of European and North American women during World War II was unthinkable in Japan, especially during wartime, when the rejection of Western ways of life was encouraged.

The emergence of the kasutori culture brought new models of relationships between Japanese men and women. The Western practice of dating became popular and activities such as dancing, going to the movies, and meeting at cafés became common activities for young couples.

The Japanese press followed suit by moving away from the wholesome wartime literature and moving toward more decadent themes. An entirely new genre called *Nikutai Bungaku* developed, characterized by the works of such authors as Tamura Taijiro, who wrote stories and essays about men finding salvation and freedom through their sexual relations with women. This new trend was easy to understand, because for many post-war

Japanese, their body was the only possession they had managed to preserve from the destruction of war.

Japan experienced a record period of economic growth from the post-war era to the end of the Cold War. This period came to be known as the Japanese Economic Miracle. Japan rapidly became the world's second largest economy, after the United States, by the 1960s.

The Economic Miracle resulted from the economic interventionism of the Japanese government and the aid the country received from the United States. Following World War II, the United States shifted its focus to the Soviet Union and other nations governed by communist parties. As a result, the United States gave preferential treatment in the form of special access to American technology, markets, and most importantly capital, to countries such as Japan and the Federal Republic of Germany in an effort to contain Communism.

The miracle years were characterized by several factors:

1. The cooperation of manufacturers, suppliers, distributors, and banks who operated in informal business groups called *keiretsu*.
2. The emergence of powerful unions.
3. The introduction of *shunto*, annual wage negotiations between the enterprise unions and the employers.
4. Good relations between business and the government bureaucrats.
5. The guarantee of lifetime employment (*Shushin koyo*) in large corporations and highly unionized blue-collar factories.

Keiretsu are a set of companies with interlocking business relationships and shareholdings. The member companies own small portions of the shares in each other's companies. This system helps insulate each company from stock market fluctuations and takeover attempts.

Shunto began in the 1940s and by the mid-1950s was a set feature in industrial relations. It was customary for the enterprise unions to begin their negotiations after the larger unions had concluded their own deals. This enabled the enterprise unions to push their own companies to match the increases set earlier and result in considerable wage increases across the board.

The period of rapid economic growth between 1955 and 1961 paved the way for the Golden Sixties. In 1965, Japan's nominal GDP (Gross domestic product) was estimated at just over $91 billion. Fifteen years later, in 1980, the nominal GDP had soared to a record $1.065 trillion.

Under the leadership of Prime Minister Ikeda, the Japanese government undertook an ambitious income doubling plan. Interest rates and taxes were lowered in an effort to motivate spending. Further, the government expanded investment in its infrastructure, building highways, high-speed railways, subways, airports, port facilities and dams.

Japan was and still is a very frugal society. The high savings rate led to rapid capital accumulation in Japan compared to other war torn countries and gave the government an extraordinary ability to spend on infrastructure projects.

The Japanese government also pushed for trade liberalization. They succeeded in removing or reducing restrictions on the free exchange of goods by securing a protected market through internal regulations that favored Japanese products and firms. By April of 1960, trade imports were 41 percent liberalized (compared to 22 percent in 1956). By the time Prime Minister Ikeda left office, the Japanese GNP (Gross national product) was growing at a phenomenal rate of 13.9 percent.

But ultimately it was the Japanese consumers who bore the brunt of shouldering the cost of Japanese companies' competition abroad, in the form of high cost of consumer goods.

During the war years, the Japanese people were taught to direct their devotion to the nation and support its military expansion. After the war, this same devotion was redirected towards the nation's economic expansion.

Time and time again, the Japanese were reminded that they were a homogeneous people, superior to all other Asians and even superior to the westerners. They were encouraged not to be too concerned about their individual well-being and to focus their efforts toward establishing their national position in the post-war world.

Finally, Japan's relations with the United States was on equal footing and the Japanese people's feeling of dependence gradually lessened, and their self-confidence increased. This gave rise to a general desire for greater independence from the United States.

As pressure began to mount in the 1950s and 1960s to close down the American military bases in Japan, the Japanese government found itself balancing left-wing pressure advocating dissociation from the United States against the country's need for military protection.

On December 18, 1956, Japan joined the United Nations. Many Japanese welcomed this step and saw it as a way of lessening the country's dependence on the United States for protection. From the late 1950s onwards Japan actively participated in the United Nation's social and economic activities. As Japan's role and contributions increased, so did the sentiment that Japan should be given a permanent seat in the UN Security Council since Japan was one of the top contributors to United Nation's peacekeeping operations. To date, Japan's seat on the Security Council remains non-permanent.

When Japan joined the United Nations, its financial contribution for peacekeeping operations was only 1.97 percent. By 2016, Japan had become the third largest contributor after the United States and China.

The approved budget for the United Nations' peacekeeping operations for the fiscal year July 1, 2016 to June 30, 2017 was $7.87 billion US. The 10 nations assessed with the highest contributions for peacekeeping operations in 2016 were:

1. United States (28.57%)
2. China (10.29%)
3. Japan (9.68%)
4. Germany (6.39%)
5. France (6.31%)
6. United Kingdom (5.80%)
7. Russian Federation (4.01%)
8. Italy (3.75%)
9. Canada (2.92%)
10. Spain (2.44%)

On January 19, 1960, the *Treaty of Mutual Cooperation and Security* was signed in Washington, revising the security treaty of 1952. The revised treaty stated that any attack perpetrated against Japan or the United States within the Japanese territorial administration required both countries to act to meet the common threat. In order to support that requirement, it was necessary for the United States to continue to maintain its military presence in Japan. The treaty was submitted to the Japanese Diet for ratification, which engendered violent opposition from Japanese leftists who sought to prevent it from being accredited.

When the House of Representatives consented to the treaty on May 20, massive demonstrations and rioting by Japanese students and trade unions followed. On June 15, 1960, a university student protesting against the treaty outside the Diet was killed by the police. This incident led to the largest demonstrations in Japanese history, against both police brutality and the treaty. As a result, the Japanese prime minister at the time, Nobusuke Kishi, requested that the United States President, Dwight D. Eisenhower, postpone his planned visit to Japan.

The treaty was passed by default on June 19, when the House of Councillors (*Sangiin*) failed to vote on the issue within the required 30 days.

On July 15, 1960, after losing face with the United States and having been unable to placate the demonstrators, Prime Minister Kishi resigned. Hayato Ikeda became the new prime minister.

Japan's post-war economic boom spurred a massive increase in the country's communications infrastructure in the 1950s. When NHK, Japan's public broadcasting station, began broadcasting television in 1953 it paved the way for the emergence of countless private broadcasting companies. Soon it was feared that Tokyo would be overrun by transmission towers.

At the same time, Japan wanted to construct a monument to symbolize its post-war achievements. An idea was eventually conceived that satisfied both needs. In Tokyo, a tower was constructed that served the support structure for an antenna and as a symbol of national pride, simultaneously.

In 1958, construction on the 332.9 meter (1,092 foot) Tokyo Tower was completed at a cost of ¥2.8 billion (USD $8.4 million in 1958). Situated in the Minato district of Tokyo, the tower served as a communications and observation tower. The design of the tower was inspired by the lattice structure of the Eiffel Tower, but it was painted white and international orange to comply with air safety regulations. It was constructed of steel, a third of which was scrap metal taken from American tanks that were damaged in the Korean War. It stands taller than the Eiffel Tower but weighs 3,300 tons less. Tokyo Tower, the symbol of Japan's recovery and success, was the tallest artificial structure in Japan until April of 2010, when the new Tokyo Skytree became the tallest building in Japan.

In 1964, Tokyo celebrated Japan's progress and reemergence on the world stage by hosting the Summer Olympics (the games of the XVIII Olympiad) from October 10 to 24. The event marked the first time that the Olympics were held in Asia. Tokyo was originally chosen to host the 1940 Summer Olympics; however, that honor was conferred on Helsinki after Japan's invasion of China.

After being designated as the host city for the 1964 Summer Olympics, Japan embarked upon an enormous modernization of

Tokyo's infrastructure to accommodate the large numbers of tourists expected to visit the city.

A great deal of energy and money were devoted to upgrading the city's physical infrastructure, including new buildings, highways, stadiums, hotels, airports, and trains. A new satellite was activated to facilitate live international broadcasts during the games. Multiple train and subway lines, a large project to build highways, and a new bullet train were completed. The Tokaido Shinkansen was inaugurated on October 1, 1964 between Tokyo and Shin Osaka. It was able to travel this distance in just four hours, making it the fastest train in the world at the time. Both Haneda International Airport and the Port of Tokyo were also modernized.

Ninety-three nations participated in the 1964 games. Athletes from East Germany and West Germany competed together, for the first time in decades, under the name the United Team of Germany.

The Olympic Flame was lit by torchbearer Yoshinori Sakai, born in Miyoshi City in the Hiroshima prefecture on August 6, 1945, the day the United States dropped the atomic bomb on the city of Hiroshima.

The event proved to be a great success for the city of Tokyo, and for Japan as a whole. The broadcast of the opening ceremony was watched by over 70% of the viewing public worldwide. The new Japan was no longer a wartime enemy, but a peaceful country that threatened no one, and this transformation was accomplished in fewer than 20 years.

Japan received another nod from the global community in 1965 when The Bureau of International Expositions chose Osaka to host the 1970 World Fair. Expo '70 was held from March 15 to September 13, 1970. The Fair's theme that year was "Progress and Harmony for Mankind." This was the first World Fair held in Japan.

Seventy-seven countries participated in the Fair, and the number of visitors surpassed 64 million people, making it one of the largest and best-attended expositions in history.

The former site of Expo '70 is currently the Expo Commemoration Park. Almost all of the Fair's structures have been demolished, but a few, such as the Tower of the Sun, the centerpiece of the fair, remain. A time capsule was left at the site, which was intended to be opened in the year 6970 A.D.

During the Allied occupation of Japan, the development of aircraft was banned. As a result, many Japanese aeronautical engineers lost their jobs. When the San Francisco Peace Treaty was signed in 1951, Japan was permitted to resume its development of aviation technology. This enabled Japan to move into the field of space exploration in the mid-1950s.

The Avionics and Supersonic Aerodynamics (AVSA) group, led by Hideo Itokawa, a pioneer of the Japanese space program at the University of Tokyo, began exploring rocket technology and succeeded in launching the Pencil Rocket on April 12, 1955. By the 1960s, two organizations, the Institute of Space and Astronautical Science (ISAS) and the National Space Development Agency of Japan (NASDA), were developing their own rockets.

Between 1966 and 1970, ISAS in partnership with Nissan produced an experimental carrier rocket called the Lambda 4S. Following four unsuccessful launches, ISAS was finally able to place the first Japanese satellite, the Osumi-5, into orbit on February 11, 1970.

In 1986, Japan agreed to participate in the International Space Station (ISS) program. The ISS is the most complex international scientific and engineering project in history and the largest structure humans have ever put in space. Five space agencies representing 15 countries built the $100 billion International Space Station and continue to operate it today. The National Aeronautics and Space Administration (NASA), Russia's Roscosmos State Corporation for Space Activities (Roscosmos), the European Space Agency, the Canadian Space Agency, and the Japan Aerospace Exploration Agency (JAXA) are the primary partners.

In 2003, ISAS and NASDA merged with the National Aerospace Laboratory of Japan (NAL) to form the Japan Aerospace Exploration Agency (JAXA).

It is clear that Japan in the post-war years has achieved extraordinary gains and has become one of the major players in both the global economic and technological arenas. Since Japan's surrender to the Allies its diplomatic policy has been based on a close partnership with the United States with the emphasis on international cooperation.

In his speech to the National Diet of Japan, Prime Minister Yasuo Fukuda (the 58th prime minister of Japan, serving from 2007 to 2008) stated, "Japan aspires to become a hub of human resource development as well as for research and intellectual contributions to further promote cooperation in the field of peace-building."

The United States returned the Bonin Islands to Japan in June of 1968, and by signing the *Okinawa Reversion Agreement* on June 17, 1971, United States also returned Okinawa to Japan.

Despite this, to date Okinawa is still host to approximately 50,000 United States military personnel and 74 percent of the American military bases in Japan. In December 2016, amidst a string of crimes committed by United States military personnel, including the murder of a 20-year-old Japanese woman, the United States agreed to return more than 9,000 acres of land on Okinawa to the Japanese government.

This relinquishment reduced the amount of American-controlled land on Okinawa by a mere 17 percent. In return, the Japanese government agreed to build new helipads for the American military's use in Okinawa, in line with the 1960 Treaty of Mutual Cooperation and Security granting the United States the right to certain defense facilities in Japan.

# THE PERSONAL SIDE OF WAR: INTERVIEWS

**Name:** Stephanie Adachi
**Birthplace:** Burbank, California

Just a few hours after the attack on Pearl Harbor, Federal Bureau of Investigation (FBI) agents, many of whom had no evidence, search warrants, or arrest warrants, went door-to-door and arrested 1,212 issei (first-generation Japanese immigrants) who were residing in Hawaii and the mainland USA.

Among those who were arrested were priests, teachers in language schools, officers of community organizations, and newspaper editors, all prominent leaders in the Japanese American communities. Subsequently, these individuals were placed in United States Justice Department internment camps located in New Mexico, North Dakota, Texas, and Montana. Some Japanese Americans were paroled to their families after receiving clearance from an Enemy Alien Hearing Board.

In the days that followed the attack, President Roosevelt issued Presidential Proclamations 2525, 2526, and 2527 authorizing the detention of allegedly dangerous enemy aliens. This resulted in the arrest of thousands of suspected individuals of Japanese, German, and Italian ancestry.

Stephanie Adachi's great-grandfather, Masazumi Adachi, was one of those arrested by the FBI. He was on the board of directors of a Japanese school called Dai-ni Gakuen. He was taken from his home without prior questioning, and his wife and daughter were terrified when they came home and discovered that he had vanished.

Masazumi Adachi was 36 years old at the time and his wife, Otomi, was 37. Their daughter, Emiko, was only sixteen. The

Adachis were from Tottori prefecture located in the Chugoku region of Japan. Their daughter Emiko was born in the United States.

Details of Stephanie's family's internment remain sketchy to this day because it was something that was not discussed very much in her family. Stephanie believes that this was because either they were ashamed of what had happened to them during World War II, or they just wanted to leave their grim memories in the past and move forward with their lives.

Otomi and Emiko were forced to report to the Santa Anita Assembly Center in Arcadia, California. Without Masazumi, they packed up their belongings as best they could. They were each allowed to bring only one suitcase; therefore, they entrusted belongings they could not bring with them to the care of their neighbors. They also buried some personal items in the backyard of their house.

Stephanie's grandmother, Emiko, often mentioned how dehumanizing it was to stay at the Santa Anita Racetrack (Assembly Center). Although there were 500 barracks constructed on the former parking lot, with a peak population of 18,719 internees, over 8,500 Japanese Americans were forced to live in converted horse stalls. Emiko and her mother resided in one of these stalls until they were transferred to the Gila River War Relocation Center, located approximately 30 miles southeast of Phoenix, Arizona.

The Gila River War Relocation Center consisted of two separate camps, Canal and Butte. Otomi and Emiko were sent to the Butte Camp. Gila River began operating on July 20, 1942. Canal Camp closed on September 28, 1945. Butte Camp was shut down on

November 10, 1945. The camp held over 13,000 internees, most of whom were from California.

During her internment at the Gila River War Relocation Center, Emiko attended school and earned her high school diploma. She also had a part-time job mending army parachutes. She saved the money she earned so she could order things from the Sears catalog.

Masazumi was sent to Tule Lake after first being imprisoned at the Tuna Canyon Detention Station. The Tuna Canyon Detention Station also held local German and Italian internees as well as Japanese Peruvians, who were all considered to be high-risk enemy aliens. On December 16, 1941, Tuna Canyon received its first enemy aliens, who had been taken into custody by the FBI. After that, it operated as a clearinghouse for the male Japanese enemy aliens arrested in Southern California.

During his internment at Tule Lake, Masazumi played baseball. For many who were incarcerated, sports served as an escape from the monotony of prison life.

Beginning in 1943, the internment camps hosted interracial baseball games. In May and June of that year, two men, Jiggs Yamada and Ship Tamai, who were interned at Tule Lake, arranged games against the Klamath Falls Pelicans and the semi-pro all-star team from Oregon. The Tulean All-Stars, as they were known, won both games by a score of 16-0 and 16-8.

Stephanie later learned that her great-grandfather had taught a Buddhist monk, who later became one of the head priests at their local Zen Buddhist temple, how to play baseball.

Although Stephanie and her parents knew that Masazumi was interned at the Tule Lake facility, they did not know that he had initially been taken to the Tuna Canyon Detention Station. It wasn't until they visited the Japanese American National Museum in Los Angeles, that was hosting an exhibition on Tuna Canyon, that they were able to find his name in the archives. Interestingly, Stephanie and her younger sister belonged to a high school golf club, and one of the courses they played on was called Verdugo Hills. Unknown to Stephanie and her sister at the time, the golf course sat on the land that housed the former Tuna Canyon Detention Station. In Stephanie's words, "…that came full circle in a way. We were playing golf on land where my great-grandfather was imprisoned. "

The golf course closed on December 31, 2016, because Snowball West Investments, L.P., the owner of the property, wanted to develop a gated residential community on the site. Currently, the Glendale-Crescenta V.O.I.C.E., a group seeking to transform the golf course into a regional park, also wants to see a portion of the land used to commemorate the site's former use as the Tuna Canyon Detention Station. A previous effort to preserve the site as a historic cultural monument failed in 2013, partly because the site's historic buildings and structures were demolished in 1960, the year the golf course opened.

Eventually, as the camps began to close down and the internees were allowed to leave, the Adachi family returned to Los Angeles to check on their possessions. The neighbors they had entrusted had kept some of their items but the personal items they had buried in the backyard were mostly gone.

The family ended up returning to Tottori after the war. Stephanie's great-grandparents were issei and could not become

American citizens by law. Emiko was born in the United States, but it is uncertain whether she was encouraged to renounce her citizenship.

They had all responded to the loyalty questionnaire. Questions 25 through 28 asked whether the individual's birth had been registered in Japan, whether the individual had renounced Japanese citizenship, whether the individual would serve in combat duty wherever ordered, and finally, whether the individual would declare loyalty to the United States and renounce allegiance to the Emperor of Japan. The Adachis had answered in a way that was deemed unfavorable by the United States government. People in this position became known as the "No-no Japanese." In most instances, the respondents elected to answer negatively to the questions, particularly as it related to renouncing their allegiance to the Emperor of Japan—because to them, renouncing implied that they previously held allegiance.

For the Adachi family, it was actually very simple. After their horrible ordeal, the family just wanted to be together again and they did not want to stay in a country that did not accept them.

In the years that followed, Emiko got married and had a daughter of her own. The family, including Emiko's parents, returned to the United States in 1953-54, just a year or two after the US military occupation of Japan had ended. Japan was in the process of rebuilding after the war—as were the members of the Adachi family.

**Name:** Seki Hanuda

**Birthplace:** Nagano Prefecture, Japan

Seki was 20 years old when the United States declared war on Japan following the bombing of Pearl Harbor. Suffering from the effects of Alzheimer's disease, she struggles to recall her experiences during the war; but there are some memories which particularly stand out for her, even at the age of 95.

She remembers going to work in a cotton mill in Nagoya, which today is the third largest city in the Chubu region. Nagoya is one of Japan's major ports, along with Tokyo, Osaka, Kobe, Yokohama, Chiba, and Kitakyushu. It has been the home of Mitsubishi Aircraft Company since 1920 and became the target of American air raids during World War II.

The first attack took place on April 18, 1942, as part of the Doolittle Raid, which mainly targeted Tokyo. A B-25 bomber dropped bombs on the Mitsubishi Aircraft Company, the Matsuhigecho Oil Warehouse, the Nagoya Castle military barracks, and the Nagoya War Industries Plant.

The bombings continued through 1945, not only targeting military installations but also inflicting a general firebombing on the city. The United States military employed single-bomber attacks on the city between the winter of 1944 and the spring of 1945 as part of the psychological warfare to disrupt the city and damage the morale of its citizens. These bombings destroyed approximately 113,000 buildings and killed more than 3,800 people.

During World War II, Nagoya was prominent in producing machine tools, bearings, railway equipment, metal alloys, tanks, motor vehicles, and processed foods.

When the government confiscated all the cotton mill machines in order to melt them down and produce weapons, Seki found herself out of work. This unfortunate turn of events turned out to be a blessing in disguise because it saved her from the subsequent Allied bombing raids.

Seki traveled from Nagoya to Tokyo and found a job as a house maid, working for one of the executives of Tokyo Shibaura Electric K.K. (which became the Toshiba Corporation in 1978). It was a job she enjoyed and her working relationship with the family was a favorable one. Unfortunately, after only six months of employment she was informed that the family could no longer keep her as a house maid. Although the family was financially well off, due to the war time food shortages, they could not afford to feed everyone. They were forced to let her go.

Japan experienced a severe food shortage both during and after the war. This was due to the disruption of food imports from the occupied territories, and the buildup of the Japanese military. Provisioning the troops was considered to be a priority, and the civilians had to make do with what was left over. For example, between 1940-41 and 1944-45, the amount of rice supplied to the armed forces rose from 161 to 744 thousand tons.

Seki left Tokyo and returned home to Nagano. There, she found work in a blacksmith shop, where she remained until she was married in 1949.

Raising a family in post-war Japan had its difficulties, but people still attempted to give life some semblance of normalcy.

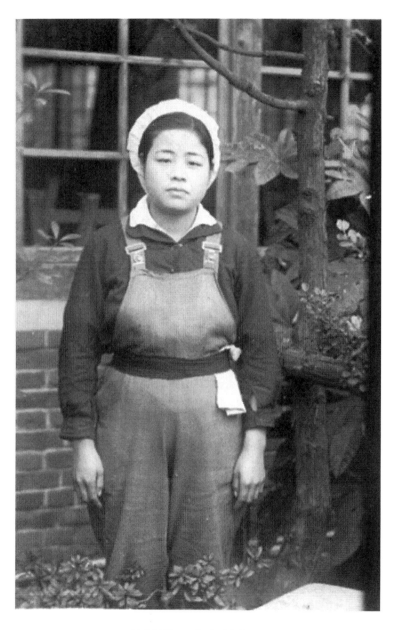

Seki Hanuda in Tokyo

Seki Hanuda in Nagano

**Name:** Aylen Hasegawa
**Birthplace:** Puyallup, Washington

Aylen Hasegawa was born on February 19, 1942, the day President Roosevelt signed Executive Order 9066 giving the military broad powers to ban any citizen from a fifty- to sixty-mile-wide coastal area stretching from Washington State to California and extending inland into southern Arizona.

The enactment of EO9066 resulted in the forceful uprooting and resettlement of approximately 120,000 Japanese Americans in one of ten permanent detention centers from 1942 to 1946. Aylen's family was among the approximately 13,000 Japanese Americans who were taken to the Minidoka Relocation Center located in Hunt, Idaho. Minidoka began receiving internees on August 10, 1942, many of whom were former residents of Washington, Oregon and Alaska.

The family was first ordered to the Puyallup Assembly Center, better known as Camp Harmony, situated at the western Washington fairgrounds in the heart of Puyallup, Washington, in May of 1942. The Hasegawa family consisted of Masuo and Betty Fumi and their three sons, Richard (age 2), Gary (age 1) and Aylen (six months old). Aylen's extended family, which included his father's two sisters and his mother, were also sent to the same temporary camp until they were transferred to Minidoka several months later. His baby brother Robert was born in 1943 at camp Minidoka.

The family was given very short notice to evacuate and they were allowed to bring only one suitcase for each family member. Betty packed most of the suitcases with diapers, since all three boys still needed them. The family had a dog, Bronco, a German Shepard mix. The animal was credited with saving their oldest son, Richard, from certain death by pulling him off the nearby railroad tracks just before the train came roaring through. Unfortunately, Bronco had to be euthanized when the family had to abandon their home—evacuees were not permitted to bring their pets with them to the internment camps.

Masuo and Betty were forced to sell all of their farm equipment and implements for just pennies on the dollar. People had heard about the evacuation and took full advantage of the situation. Masuo also lost his brand new truck and the entire crop harvest.

Although Masuo and Betty thought the attacks on Pearl Harbor were terrible and shocking, they were very surprised by the government's order to evacuate. They were American citizens by birth and could not comprehend how the American government could treat its own people in this manner.

Masuo had never been to Japan and only spoke a little Japanese to communicate with his mother. Betty was born in Seattle on October 23, 1917. However, due to her father's illness, her family had moved to Osaka when she was just six years old. Betty attended school in Japan for six years (grammar school in Osaka, and the Imperial Girls' School in Tokyo) before being sent back to the United States along with her sister, Lilyan, while their parents and younger brother remained behind. Understandably, Betty was fluent in Japanese.

The family planned to reunite in America; however, that never came to pass as Betty's father died in Japan. When the war broke out Betty's parents and younger brother were living in Tokyo. Betty's brother, David, was regarded with distrust by the Japanese authorities because he had been born in the United States.

Eventually he was jailed on the suspicion of being a spy. In Aylen's words, "It seems this family was in trouble no matter in which country they resided."

Camp Harmony was comprised of four distinct areas. Area A was located northeast of the fairgrounds and housed approximately 2,000 internees. Area B was east of the fairgrounds and home to approximately 1,200 displaced Japanese Americans. Area C was situated northwest of the fairgrounds and accommodated 800 residents. Area D was located on the fairgrounds proper, which included the racetrack and the grandstands, east of the roller coaster. Area D was the largest section of Camp Harmony, housing approximately 3,000 internees. Aylen's family was living in Area D in what he described as a converted horse stable.

When the family relocated to Minidoka, they were consigned to one end of a military style barracks. These barracks had tar paper sheathing on the walls, which permitted wind and dust to come inside, covering everything. Like all other camps at the time, there was no privacy. The camp residents used communal latrines and ate in communal mess halls.

Betty worked tirelessly as a nurse in the camp hospital while her mother-in-law and sisters-in-law watched the boys. It was during this busy time when Robert was born.

While the family was detained at the camp, Aylen's uncles, Eddie Watanabe and Shig Sumioka, were serving in the war as members of the 442nd Regimental Combat Team. In addition, Aylen's great-uncle, Professor Henry Tatsumi, was helping the war effort by teaching Japanese language skills to American GIs at the University of Washington Department of Far Eastern Languages.

Professor Tatsumi helped to set up the Navy Japanese Language School for the United States Military Intelligence Service (MIS) in Boulder, Colorado and Ann Arbor, Michigan.

Aylen and his brothers were just infants when their family was sent to the internment camp in Idaho. Aylen was delivered by Dr. Charles Aylen, who insisted that Betty deliver her child in his clinic in Puyallup. This happened during the time when all Japanese were under strict curfew. Dr. Aylen was, in fact, defying curfew and putting himself at risk by helping to deliver the baby at his clinic. According to Aylen, the doctor's actions were, "A courageous act that reflected a true sense of compassion and a physician's calling," at a time when many Americans had surrendered to fear and prejudice.

The Hasegawa family ran a successful 160 acre farm in Puyallup. They grew hops, rhubarb, and strawberries. But since their land was leased, the family ended up losing everything after the war.

Masuo's parents were issei, born in Japan, and by law they were ineligible for United States' citizenship and consequently barred from owning land. They did not consider purchasing the land under the name of their son, who was nisei and a US citizen by birth.

Following their internment, the family did not have a home or a livelihood to return to in Washington. However, in 1943, Masuo took advantage of an opportunity for early release from Minidoka by accepting a sponsored relocation to the Midwest. He traveled to Rockford, Illinois alone, leaving his family behind in an attempt to set things up for his wife and children in anticipation of their release. At that time, the West Coast was still considered a military zone and Japanese Americans were barred from returning to their former homes.

Betty and her sons left Minidoka in September of 1944 and traveled to Rockford to join Masuo. Masuo had been working three jobs, trying to earn enough money to purchase a home for his family. When Betty arrived, the tenants in the house Masuo had purchased refused to move out. They claimed that they would not move out because some "dirty Japs" were moving in. Fortunately for Betty and the boys, a neighbor, Myrtle Cavanaugh, saw the distraught family on the sidewalk and came out to investigate. Once she understood the situation, she asked her husband, Captain Ed Cavanaugh of the Rockford Police Department, to assist. It took nearly a month to evict the "obstinate squatters." The Hasegawa family finally moved into their first owned home.

The Hasegawa family eventually settled in the South Side Kenwood neighborhood of Chicago, Illinois. Betty, who had been trained as a registered nurse at Columbus Hospital from 1936 to 1939, worked as a nurse at the University of Chicago Hospitals. Every Thanksgiving she invited the medical students for a holiday meal. According to her son Gary, "She just didn't like to see anybody be by themselves on a holiday, especially at Thanksgiving and Christmas."

In the 1980s, Betty Hasegawa was one of the 750 people who testified in Washington before the Commission on Wartime Relocation and Internment of Civilians. These hearings were referred to as the Redress Hearings and ultimately resulted in a formal apology by the government and the payment of reparations to more than 82,200 Japanese Americans. Gary Hasegawa stated, "She did . . . it mainly for an apology--until then, no one even acknowledged that taking US citizens and putting them behind barbed wire was outrageous."

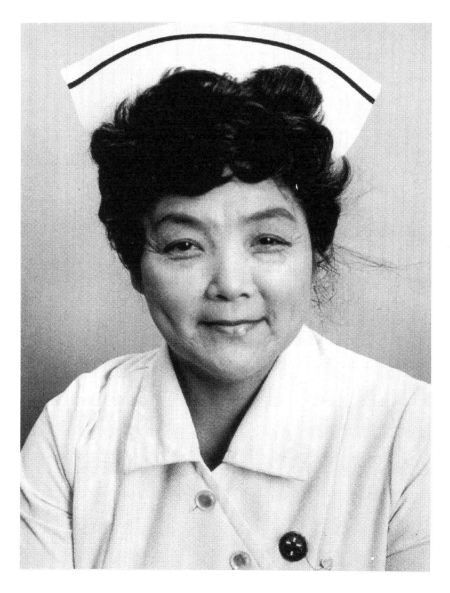

Betty Hasegawa

BUDGET BUREAU NO. 53-R045-43

(LOCAL BOARD DATE STAMP WITH CODE)

## STATEMENT OF UNITED STATES CITIZEN OF JAPANESE ANCESTRY

1. Hasegawa     Masuo
      (Surname)      (English given name)      (Japanese given name)

   (a) Alias    none

2. Local selective service board    #1 Tribune Bldg.
                                           (Number)

    Puyallup      Pierce      Wash.
       (City)          (County)         (State)

3. Date of birth   June 2, 1914     Place of birth   Vashon, Washington

4. Present address    16-2-2      Hunt      Idaho
                    (Street)         (City)        (State)

5. Last two addresses at which you lived 3 months or more (exclude residence at relocation center and at assembly center):

    Rt. 2 Box 177, Puyallup, Wash.     From 19.3   To 1942

    Rt. 2, Box 346, Puyallup, Wash.     From 1928   To 1933

6. Sex   Male     Height   70     Weight   155

7. Are you a registered voter?   Yes    Year first registered   1934

   Where? Alderton, Wash.     Party   Democrat

8. Marital status   Married     Citizenship of wife   U. S. A.    Race of wife   Japanese

9. Hasegawa, Hisao (deceased)   Kumamoto    Japan
      (Father's Name)      (Town or Ken)    (Birthplace)    (State or Country)    (Occupation)

10. Deguchi, Tatsuye    Kumamoto    Japan    Farm
      (Mother's Name)      (Town or Ken)    (Birthplace)    (State or Country)    (Occupation)

In items 11 and 12, you need not list relatives other than your parents, your children, your brothers and sisters. For each person give name; relationship to you (such as father); citizenship; complete address; occupation.

11. Relatives in the United States (if in military service, indicate whether a selectee or volunteer):

   (a) Hasegawa, Tatsuye     Mother     Japanese
            (Name)      (Relationship to you)      (Citizenship)

     14-12-E, Hunt, Idaho     Farm
      (Complete address)      (Occupation)      (Volunteer or selectee)

   (b) Hasegawa, Betty     Wife     U. S. A.
            (Name)      (Relationship to you)      (Citizenship)

     16-2-E, Hunt, Idaho     Housewife
      (Complete address)      (Occupation)      (Volunteer or selectee)

   (c) Hasegawa, Richard     Son    U. S. A.
            (Name)      (Relationship to you)      (Citizenship)

     16-2-E, Hunt, Idaho     School
      (Complete address)      (Occupation)      (Volunteer or selectee)

DSS Form 301A        (If additional space is necessary, attach sheets)       16—32565-1
(1-23-43)

## The "Loyalty" Questionnaire

23. List contributions you have made to any society, organization, or club:

| Organization | Place | Amount | Date |
|---|---|---|---|
| J. A. C. L. | Puyallup, Wash. | $5.00 | 1939 |
| Red Cross | Puyallup, Wash. | $5.00 | 1942 |

24. List magazines and newspapers to which you have subscribed or have customarily read:

Popular Photography, Parents, Tacoma Tribune, Seattle Times, Pacific Citizen, Japanese American Courier.

25. To the best of your knowledge, was your birth ever registered with any Japanese governmental agency for the purpose of establishing a claim to Japanese citizenship? __Yes__

(a) If so registered, have you applied for cancelation of such registration? __Yes__
(Yes or no)

When? __Cancelled 1934__ Where? __Seattle, Wash.__

26. Have you ever applied for repatriation to Japan? __No__

27. Are you willing to serve in the armed forces of the United States on combat duty, wherever ordered? __Yes__

28. Will you swear unqualified allegiance to the United States of America and faithfully defend the United States from any or all attack by foreign or domestic forces, and forswear any form of allegiance or obedience to the Japanese emperor, or any other foreign government, power, or organization? __Yes__

| __Feb. 15, 1943__ | | __S/ Masuo Hasegawa__ |
|---|---|---|
| (Date) | | (Signature) |

NOTE.—Any person who knowingly and wilfully falsifies or conceals a material fact or makes a false or fraudulent statement or representation in any matter within the jurisdiction of any department or agency of the United States is liable to a fine of not more than $10,000 or 10 years' imprisonment, or both.

U. S. GOVERNMENT PRINTING OFFICE   16—32565-1

The "Loyalty" Questionnaire (Page 2)

WAR RELOCATION AUTHORITY

WASHINGTON

FEB 27 1943

To Mr. Otto Reise

Rt. 2

Puyallup, Washington

Dear Sir:

Masuo Hasegawa _____ has given your name as a reference in connection with an application to leave a relocation center of this Authority for employment, education, or residence elsewhere.

We should appreciate it if you would give us your opinion of this individual with respect to such matters as the extent of Americanization through education and upbringing, general standing and reputation in the community, and occupational abilities. If you have ever employed the applicant, a statement concerning the quality of the work performed for you would be helpful.

An addressed envelope which needs no postage is enclosed for your reply.

Sincerely yours,

*D. S. Myer*

Director

In reply,
please refer to:
Hasegawa, Masuo
#12117
Minidoka, W. R. A.
16 - 2 # E
Enclosure

*Dear Sirs:- I have lived neighbor to Masuo Hasegawa for a number of years and believe him to be a real american, very conscientous trustworthy hardworking and having a real desire to live according to american standards*
*Yours truly Otto Reise*

Recommendation Letter for Masuo Hasegawa

152

**Name:**      **Curt Hasegawa**

**Birthplace:**   **Island of Hawaii (The Big Island), Hawaii**

When President Roosevelt established the 442nd Regimental Combat Team on February 1, 1943, Hawaii-born nisei (second generation Japanese Americans) made up about two-thirds of the regiment. Many of the boys living in Hawaii enlisted to fight for America as soon as the war broke out in an effort to prove their loyalty.

Curt Hasegawa is a sansei (third generation Japanese American) born on the Island of Hawaii (The Big Island). His great-uncle was a decorated member of the 442nd Regimental Combat Team, which was comprised entirely of American soldiers of Japanese ancestry. Growing up, Curt heard many stories about the war and the 442nd from his great-uncle.

In his role as a storyteller, Curt's great-uncle wanted to instill in his nephew a sense of appreciation for the sacrifices people made to ensure a better life for their families and future generations. He also wanted Curt to use the wisdom and experiences imparted to him as a guide in his life. Curt began to learn about his great-uncle's experiences when he was only ten years old, and the stories continued until he was eighteen years of age.

Curt's great-uncle was stationed at Camp Shelby, where he had done his basic training. Located in southern Mississippi just south of Hattiesburg, Camp Shelby has a long history as a basic training facility for soldiers during World War I, World War II, and all subsequent wars up to Operation Desert Storm. During World War II, Camp Shelby consisted of 360,000 acres with an additional 400,000 acres leased for maneuvers. Initially, troops were housed in tents, forming the largest tent city in the world. Later, at a cost of $24 million, 1,800 buildings were constructed at the camp.

Before World War I, Camp Shelby was home to the 37th and 38th Divisions. During World War II, those divisions were joined by the 31st, 43rd, 65th, and 69th Divisions, as well as the 442nd Regimental Combat Team. The camp also hosted units of the Women's Army Corps, a large convalescent hospital, and a prisoner of war camp. At one point, the population at Camp Shelby exceeded 100,000 troops, making it the largest training center in the world.

Initially, the mainland-born Japanese American soldiers, loosely referred to as *kotonks* by the Hawaii-born Japanese American soldiers, did not get along and fights broke out. However, in time, as these men were confronted with racial prejudice from the non-Japanese soldiers, they bonded and became good friends.

Curt's great-uncle related many incidents of having to face racial prejudice not only on the base but also out on the battlefields and from the general public. As a result, fights would break out on a regular basis between the Japanese American soldiers and the non-Japanese soldiers. Curt recalled, "My uncle talked about times when they would be out on the town for R&R and regular citizens on the street would call them names and spit on them-— while in uniform!" Indeed, these were difficult times for all Japanese Americans, both soldiers and civilians, facing hatred and prejudice from their fellow Americans.

After basic training, Curt's great-uncle was sent to Italy to fight on the battlefields. Curt remembered his great-uncle telling him about the times when his unit was dug into foxholes for the night and no one could sleep as they would hear the "shoop" sound of mortars being launched by the Germans and each soldier would be counting down the seconds before the explosion. In the darkness of night, and in their own foxholes, they would silently keep track of how close or how far their unit was as a target. Curt also remembered being told, "You wouldn't know what fear was until you were there and you realized that you might not live through the night!" Curt's great-uncle lost his best friend on the battlefield in Italy and often felt that he too should never have returned home because his friend didn't.

Curt recalled an instance when he was about 12 years of age and was a fan of war movies on television. His great-uncle asked him if he wanted to join the army. Curt said, "I responded 'yes' to the question, and told him that I wanted to be like the brave soldiers whose heroic deeds saved the day! My uncle told me that what I was referring to was Hollywood stuff, and 'real war' was scary and horrific."

When the war concluded, Curt's great-uncle returned home and started a family. He became a painting contractor, a profession he pursued for 30-plus years. He was awarded the Purple Heart as well as other medals for his valiant efforts in the war. It was a bittersweet honor, as he was proud to have served in the United States Army yet he was torn because he knew all too well what earning such medals entailed. He had demonstrated his loyalty to his country by enlisting and fighting in the 442nd. He understood that the real price of earning such medals was the blood, sweat, tears, and lives of human beings, regardless of what side of the war they were on.

The medals mysteriously disappeared after Curt's great-uncle passed away in 1987 at the age of 75. Curt believes that his great-uncle meant what he said about not being proud of earning medals for killing people and thinks that his great-uncle probably disposed of the medals prior to his death.

In the end, Curt concluded, "After many storytelling sessions with my uncle over the years, one of his last lessons to me was simply that war is just bad. There is no good side to war because it only means one thing — people could not work together to resolve their differences."

**Name:**        Shinichi Nakanishi
**Birthplace:**   Hiroshima Prefecture, Japan

A retired university professor, Shinichi Nakanishi resides in Onomichi City, located just 89 km (55 miles) east of Hiroshima City. It is his mother's hometown, and although it was not directly affected when the United States dropped the atomic bomb on Hiroshima on August 6, 1945, Onomichi City played a role both during the war and in the war's aftermath.

Facing the Seto Inland Sea, Onomichi is known as a maritime city, home to various corporations in the maritime industry, including shipbuilding companies, marine equipment manufacturers, and shipping companies. On March 28, 2005, two towns, Mukaishima and Mitsugi, were merged with Onomichi. Mukaishima was home to the Hiroshima Prisoner of War Sub-Camp No. 4 from November 1942 to September 1945. There were over 90 POW camps throughout Japan that housed approximately 36,000 prisoners of war. In Mukaishima, the number of POWs, both British and American, totaled 210. These prisoners were forced to work at the Hitachi Zosen shipyard. The Hitachi Zosen Corporation was originally known as Osaka Iron Works. The company primarily produced minesweepers, landing craft, and cargo transport submarines, and converted old merchant ships for military use. They acquired the Mukaishima shipyard in 1943.

Shinichi's grandfather, Hideaki Aoyama, was a corpsman in the Japanese Imperial Army assigned to the POW camp in Mukaishima. Aoyama was missing his left eye; therefore, he could not fight on the battlefields. Prior to joining the army, Aoyama worked for a seaweed wholesaler. He had dreams of becoming a teacher, but his physical impairment prevented him from realizing his dreams. He learned to speak English on his own, and by doing so, he earned an assignment at the POW camp as a translator. His duties included conversing with the prisoners about health issues, and relaying their requests to his superiors, gathering information from the prisoners regarding the American and British forces, and supervising the prisoners who labored at the Hitachi Zosen shipyard.

During a conversation Aoyama had with his sister, Shinichi's aunt, he stated that the conditions at the camp were less than ideal, especially with regard to food and healthcare. After all, due to the provisioning of its military forces, Japan's resources were stretched thin during the war and its own citizens had to make do with severe shortages, as did the prisoners of war.

The people of Mukaishima had not come in contact with foreigners prior to the establishment of the POW camp in their town. Naturally, they were fearful of the foreign soldiers but at the same time the Mukaishimans were fascinated by the foreigners' fair skin and light colored eyes. The children of the town in particular expressed boundless curiosity and would visit the camp regularly to observe the prisoners. As Shinichi described it, it was almost as if they were visiting a zoo to see animals they had never seen before.

Today, there is a small memorial marking the place where the POW camp once stood. A grocery store called Every stands where the Allied prisoners of war were once imprisoned. The original monument was established in 1998 within the Mukaishima Bouseki (spinning factory) and listed the names of the twenty-three English POWs who died at the camp as a result of illness. The factory went bankrupt in 2011, forcing the townspeople to rebuild the monument at its current location, with one difference: the name of one American POW who also died at the camp was added.

Shinichi's uncle was a pharmacist so he was not drafted into the military. The Japanese government needed individuals with medical and pharmaceutical knowledge to assist at home. Shinichi's friend's father was sent to fight in Manchuria and often talked about the cruelty he suffered at the hands of the Soviets after being captured. By the end of World War II, there were between 560,000 to 760,000 Japanese POWs in the Soviet Union and Mongolia working in labor camps.

Shinichi's grandmother, Tomie Aoyama, often talked about her wartime experiences. Her family home was located near a mountaintop and when the atomic bomb was dropped, she saw a bright light in the sky. The older generation of Japanese residing in Hiroshima called it *pikadon*, meaning flash bomb. Because of his ability to speak English, Hideaki was sent to Hiroshima City to assist the survivors after the bombing. He was joined by other Japanese soldiers who were similarly tasked. No one had any knowledge of the type of environment they were being sent to.

Until August 6, 1945, Hiroshima City was generally left untouched by the unremitting Allied bombings. The reason for this was that the United States wanted an accurate measurement of the atomic bomb's effect. In the aftermath, the city was nothing more than a charred plain with a few concrete structures left standing. There were corpses scattered everywhere, and for those who managed to survive the blast, medical treatment was virtually nonexistent. Many of the city's medical facilities were located near the hypocenter, and only a few doctors remained.

There were chaos and confusion, and many unfounded rumors surfaced as a result. One was that the hibakusha, the atomic bomb survivors, were poisoned by the bomb blast, and therefore they should not be touched. For the average citizen, information about the bomb was very limited. They did not realize that some of the illnesses they were observing were the result of radiation exposure. They mistakenly thought that the bomb dropped on Hiroshima emitted a strange poison.

With nowhere left to call home, the hibakusha departed from Hiroshima City and settled elsewhere, including Onomichi City. They faced deprivation and discrimination almost anywhere they went. Some settled in the shanty towns that sprung up in Hiroshima, often known as the A-bomb slums. One of these slums was located along the banks of the Otagawa River, and the other was in Fukushima-cho, just west of the river. Fortunately, in Onomichi no such slum existed and the few hibakusha that lived there were able to work regular jobs and lead a normal life. Still, they were the object of curiosity among Onomichi's citizens.

As an educator, Shinichi is discouraged by the fact that the younger Japanese today are unaware of Hiroshima's post-war history. He pointed out that many hibakusha became *kataribe*, or storytellers reminding people of the horrors of nuclear war by writing about their experiences and speaking in public. There have also been various *mangas* (comics) written about the subject. Two prominent artists, Fumiyo Kono and Yuka Nishioka, have attempted to portray the extraordinary tragedies in Hiroshima and Nagasaki in their works. The two artists, are in fact, non-hibakusha. Shinichi believes that these mangas and books could be used to educate the young, but  sadly they are often not permitted in schools due to their graphic nature.

In 1950, Shinichi's grandfather was diagnosed with lung cancer. He passed away in 1955 at the age of 43, leaving behind a nine year old daughter, Shinichi's mother. Although the family believes that he might have developed cancer as a result of being in Hiroshima City after the bomb was dropped, his case was never properly documented to prove that it was associated with the radiation exposure from the bomb. Until that point in time, no one had ever studied the effects of exposure on the scale delivered by atomic weapons. Further, information and medical data about the bomb and its effects were censored or confiscated by the Occupation authorities until the early 1950s, leaving Japanese doctors mystified.

When Emperor Hirohito's surrender speech was broadcast in Onomichi, very few people could understand what was being said. Known as the Jewel Voice Broadcast, the *Imperial Rescript on the Termination of War* was delivered in the formal, classical Japanese language that only a few ordinary citizens could understand. It was the first time the emperor's voice was heard by ordinary Japanese citizens, who revered the emperor as a god. His high-pitched voice with its strange tempo seemed odd to many people. Some people refused to believe it was actually their emperor who was speaking. The broadcast was followed by an explanation, in which the people were informed that Japan had surrendered. Most of the citizens in Onomichi, like elsewhere in Japan, could not believe it. Some expressed anger while others simply cried. As a result of this broadcast, the people of Onomichi felt as though their belief system had been shattered; their emperor was not a god but a human after all, and they had lost their "country of the god."

This feeling of loss was further compounded by fear. Shinichi's family thought about what had happened in Hiroshima and Nagasaki, and they feared a third bomb would be dropped on Japan. They, along with everyone else living in Japan at the time, turned their thoughts to how to continue living and how to survive in post-war Japan.

**Name:**       Masayuki Ohkubo
**Birthplace:** Nagano Prefecture, Japan

When the San Francisco Peace Treaty was signed on September 8, 1951, it marked the end of the Allied occupation of Japan. Japan's independence was restored on April 28, 1952, and as the 1950s progressed, Japan became a Western ally and aspects of American culture became woven into the fabric of the Japanese culture.

It was during this time that Masayuki Ohkubo was born in Shinonoi, a town located in the Sarashina district of Nagano prefecture, in the Chubu region of Japan.

His father worked as a truck driver for the Meiji Milk Company. He supplemented his income by delivering papers for the Shinonoi Newspaper Distribution Center. His mother was a housewife and a farmer, tending to the family's rice field and apple orchard daily. She also spent the day taking care of the *honke* (the main family ancestral home), typically inherited by the oldest child in the family.

Masayuki's father was one of four children. There were three boys and one girl, who was the eldest child. Incidentally, it was the eldest of the boys who inherited the honke as girls were traditionally excluded from doing so.

Masayuki was the youngest of two children; his brother Yukio was two years older.

While many Japanese living in the densely populated metropolitan centers dealt with severe food shortages after the war, those living in the countryside were better off as they were relatively self-sufficient. The Ohkubos were no exception as they grew their own vegetables and kept their own milk cows. Meat and fish were readily available for purchase at the market but were priced beyond most people's means.

Most post-war families did without extravagances such as toys and candy for their children. But children being children, those living in Masayuki's village managed to construct their own toys from items they found lying around.

The three major car companies in Japan at the time were Toyota, Datsun, and Mazda. There were also a handful of smaller auto manufacturers who were producing cars, but not many people were able to purchase a vehicle at that time.

Masayuki's father drove a very utilitarian Kurogane 3-Wheeler truck. The truck was manufactured by the Nippon Jidosha Company in Tokyo. The company first introduced the 3-Wheeler truck in 1928 under the name, "New Era." These vehicles were rather unique as the front end was a motorcycle powered by a single cylinder engine. In 1937, the name was changed from New Era to *Kurogane* (black steel).

During World War II, the company halted production of the 3-Wheelers and started manufacturing 4x4 military scout cars. Production of the Kurogane resumed in 1949 and lasted until 1962, when the firm went bankrupt.

The Ohkubos were also better off financially during the post-war years because apple production yielded double the income an average salary man earned working in the city.

Those living in Nagano prefecture were rather fortunate, as they were spared by the Allied bombers, who targeted the major

Japanese cities and manufacturing zones. The Allies did manage to bomb some of the railway lines in the area; however, the homes and businesses were left untouched.

The Ohkubo family would gather around the breakfast table every morning and listen to the radio while eating their morning meal. Breakfast and other meals of the day were rather simple, consisting primarily of miso soup, rice, and pickles. On rare occasions, the family would enjoy the luxury of adding tofu, meat, or fish to their meals.

Every household in the village owned a radio during the 1950s. Radio broadcasts featured the news, music, and dramas. The Ohkubos purchased their first television set in 1962. There were only two television sets in the entire village of 1,000 residents back then! Masayuki vividly recalls the time when ten to twenty neighbors crowded into his family's home to watch the wedding of Prince Akihito and Princess Michiko (Heisei Emperor and Empress) being televised.

During Masayuki's grade school days, many American movies were televised in Japan. His first perception of Americans and life in the United States came from these early movies. This was also the case for many other Japanese living during that time period, who imagined every American being well-off, wearing stylish clothes, living in luxurious houses, and driving expensive cars.

Masayuki's father was initially drafted into the Imperial Army but was discharged for having a bad knee.

Traditionally, the Japanese conscription laws required every male to register for military service at age 20 and serve for two years. After their service they remained on reserve status, and subject to

165

recall, until age 40. Firstborn sons, students, and teachers were exempt from being drafted.

As the military situation became more grave during World War II, Japan began altering its original conscription laws. In the fall of 1943, all males over 20, including college students, were subject to the draft. In 1944, men under 20 (some as young as 15) were eligible for military service. On February 26, 1945, the laws were further updated. Men aged 15 to 60 and women aged 17 to 40 were subject to training for a projected final defense of the homeland if Japan was invaded.

Korean and Taiwanese (Formosan) citizens had been allowed to volunteer for service since 1938, but they were almost always relegated to the labor battalions. In 1944, Japan began drafting Koreans into service and expanded the draft to include the Taiwanese (Formosans) in 1945.

Masayuki's uncle was a member of the Military Police Corps, known as the Kempeitai. The Kempeitai was formed in 1881 and was active until 1945. The Corps functioned less like the conventional military police and more like the Gestapo of Nazi Germany. Although considered to be an arm of the Imperial Japanese Army, the Kempeitai also performed the duties of the military police for the Imperial Japanese Navy, the executive police under the direction of the Interior Minister, and the judicial police under the Justice Minister.

The Kempeitai was responsible for preserving peace and acting as the military police for the Imperial Army in Korea from 1907 to 1910, when Japan officially annexed Korea under the *Japan–Korea Annexation Treaty*.

The Kempeitai members were rather notorious for their brutality, not only in the occupied territories of Japan but within Japan itself as well. During World War II, Prime Minister Hideki Tojo used the Kempeitai to ensure that everyone was loyal to the war. Tojo had been the former Commander of the Kempeitai in Manchuria from 1935 to 1937.

The Kempeitai was also responsible for maintaining the Allied prisoner of war system, in which the captives were often treated with extreme cruelty. These abuses were documented in the Japanese war crimes trials, and it was estimated that there were 36,000 regular members of the Kempeitai at the end of the war.

The viciousness of the Kempeitai extended to civilians as well. Following the Doolittle Raid on Tokyo in 1942, the Kempeitai were responsible for carrying out reprisals against thousands of Chinese civilians and captured airmen.

On October 10, 1943, in response to the Allied raid on Singapore Harbor, the Kempeitai launched what is referred to as the Double Tenth Massacre, in which fifty-seven civilians were arrested and tortured on mere suspicion of their involvement in the raid.

When the war ended, twenty-one of the Kempeitai involved in the massacre were charged with war crimes. Eight received the death sentence, seven were acquitted, and the remainder were given prison sentences varying from one year to life.

Masayuki's uncle was originally stationed in Shanghai, and was later promoted and transferred to the headquarters in Nanking, the former capital of the Republic of China. On December 13, 1937, during the Second Sino-Japanese War, an episode of mass murder and mass rape committed by Japanese troops against the residents of Nanking took place. The incident occurred over a period of six weeks and involved Chinese civilians and combatants numbering over 300,000.

Masayuki's cousin was born in Nanking and the family returned to Japan in February 1946, when the baby was only 18 days old. Upon arrival, Masayuki's uncle learned that if they had arrived at the returning ship 30 minutes later, they would have all been captured and killed as all the *kempei* (the name for the individual members of the corps) were on a wanted list.

Masayuki's father had a younger brother who suffered from tuberculosis and had to be segregated during the war. Fortunately, the family's financial position helped them secure the penicillin necessary for his survival. After regaining his health, he graduated from Meiji University and secured a position with the Japanese National Tax Agency, the equivalent of the Internal Revenue Service in the United States.

After World War II, it was common to see veterans wandering the streets still wearing their uniforms.

Masayuki recalled these scenes while visiting his mother's honke during the New Year holidays. There were various festivals held at the shrine during this time and some of these veterans, still dressed in their military uniforms, were lined up along the road leading to the shrine, begging for money. Masayuki remembered that some were missing limbs. Gradually, these people ceased to come to the shrine and by 1960-1961 they had all but disappeared.

Although there were 350,000 United States personnel stationed throughout Japan during the seven year military occupation, there were no foreigners in and around Shinonoi for many years and no account of what relationships with the native Japanese would have been like, if there had been foreigners stationed or living in the area.

The Kurogane

**Name:** Diana Portugal
**Birthplace:** Fort Devens, Shirley, Massachusetts

Diana Portugal was born at Fort Devens in Shirley, Massachusetts in 1955. A United States Army Reserve military installation, Fort Devens was constructed in 1917 and served as a training and reception center during the various wars the United States participated in (World War I – Iraq Wars). Fort Devens also served as a prisoner of war camp for German and Italian prisoners from 1944 to 1946 and was designated as a detention center for enemy aliens of Italian, German and Japanese descent in 1942. It was home to the 7th Infantry Regiment and the 3rd Infantry Division from 1946 to 1950. During the Korean War (June 25, 1950 – July 27, 1953), a battalion from Fort Devens was re-designated as the Third Battalion, Eighth Cavalry Regiment and sent to Korea to join the 1st Cavalry Division. The 7th Infantry was deployed to San Francisco and sailed for Japan on August 20, 1950. Diana was the daughter of Frank Campos, a Staff Sergeant in the United States Army, and Yukie Campos, a war bride from Yokohama, Japan. During the post-war occupation of Japan, Yokohama served as a major transshipment base for American supplies and personnel, particularly during the Korean War. As the Cold War dominated the United States' foreign policy following World War II, the United States extended security commitments to two nations in Northeast Asia: South Korea and Japan. Consequently, the US accelerated its attempts to make Japan a prosperous ally.

Diana's father, Frank, was of Mexican descent and served during the Korean War. Born in Selma, California, he was the second youngest of five brothers, all of whom served in the United States military. He joined the service after graduating from high school and served for 13 years. Frank and Yukie met at a party with other soldiers and ended up living together for approximately two

171

years. Yukie told her mother that she was living with her aunt in another city at the time. Frank and Yukie had two other children, a daughter born at Fort Monmouth in Monmouth County, New Jersey in 1954 and a son who was born in 1948. There was some controversy regarding their son, however. Diana recalls finding adoption papers indicating that her father had adopted Yukie's son. Yukie explained that she was the boy's babysitter and his parents had relocated to Maine and could not take their son with them. Hence, they left the boy with her. Diana's brother remembered being called George Hatch and Diana thinks that perhaps he was her mother's illegitimate son. Perhaps he was the son of one of the servicemen in Japan during the occupation. The children born to American servicemen and Japanese women were estimated to number 5,000 to 10,000 by 1952.

When some of the war brides from Japan came to the United States, they were forced to change their names to American names and they were not allowed to wear their traditional kimonos. Diana's mother kept her Japanese name, and as Diana recalled, she never wore a kimono. She never attended the bride schools which were offered at some of the military bases to learn how to do things the American way.

The family moved to a small agricultural town in Sanger, California in 1959. Following his retirement from the military, Frank became a farm worker although he did engage in janitorial and cooking work as well. Diana's mother worked in the fruit packing houses that processed peaches, nectarines, plums, and grapes. She worked three seasons of the year and collected unemployment during the winter season when there were no crops to be packed. The packing houses also employed other Japanese women. Diana recalled going into their lunchroom on errands and seeing a room full of thin Japanese women, all speaking Japanese. Diana admitted that she felt envious of their ability to speak Japanese. Diana's mother also supplemented the family's income by sewing bridal gowns. Yukie had attended seamstress school in Japan and learned how to sew.

Diana recollected that her upbringing as a child was strict and disciplined. She and her siblings were taught how to make their beds in the military style with four corners at a time when fitted sheets did not exist, and they always had to answer respectfully. If their father was in a foul mood, they had to address him as "sir." When he was in a good mood, they called him "daddy." Although Diana's father was a second generation Mexican American, he did not identify with the Hispanic culture. The children were raised as Japanese children. Diana and her siblings were taught to work hard, they learned about the various Japanese traditions such as *Obon*, and they frequently visited Fresno's West Side to watch subtitled Japanese films. They listened to Japanese folk tales in the evening, were taught how to bow respectfully, and learned quite a few Japanese words and phrases which they eventually forgot. Diana's mother would jokingly tell Diana that she would never make a good Japanese child because she talked too much.

Yukie returned to Japan to visit her family and friends when Diana was 18 years old. After that, she planned to go back every two years and managed to visit again when Diana was 20. Unfortunately, Yukie was unable to make the third trip to Japan. She passed away unexpectedly due to cardiac arrest. She was only 48 years old.

Diana believes that her mother's untimely death was the result of pushing herself too hard. Yukie was so focused on returning to Japan for visits that she would put in 12-hour shifts each day at the packing houses. By this time, she had started to work at the orange packing house during the winter months.

How difficult it must have been for her to return to Japan after such a long absence, Diana wonders. Yukie's mother was 82 years old when Yukie returned home the first time. She spent two months in Japan, and when she came back to the United States, she experienced complete culture shock. Things seemed so different to her; even the Japanese manner of slurping noodles was completely foreign. Although she maintained her Japanese values and traditions, it appears that Yukie had adapted to the American lifestyle after all those years in the United States.

Yukie Campos

The Campos Family

**Name:**     Hiroto Sakamoto
**Birthplace:**  Okayama, Japan

Hiroto Sakamoto resides in Okayama City, located 86 miles (138 kilometers) east of Hiroshima City. Okayama is actually situated midway between the cities of Osaka and Hiroshima. Okayama City was founded in 1889 and served as the home for the Imperial Japanese Army's 17th Division base camp during World War II. Consequently, it became the target of an attack by the United States Army Air Forces on June 29, 1945. Incendiary bombs burned nearly 70% of the city, killed more than 1,700 people, and resulted in the loss of 12,000 households.

Today, the former base camp houses Okayama University. Known as the Tsushima Campus, it is one of the largest open campuses in Japan. The occupation forces utilized the Tsushima camp until 1947, after which the students of the Sixth Higher School, whose buildings were burnt down during the war, guarded the camp and resided in the former military barracks. Eventually, the camp was transformed into a campus and the faculties of Okayama University, with the exception of the Medical School, were gradually relocated to the Tsushima Campus.

Hiroto's maternal grandfather, Ryotaro, was born in Niimi City in Okayama prefecture to a wealthy family engaged in farming. When he was young he fell from a tree and became very sickly from that point on. Consequently, he failed to pass the military's physical fitness test.

Ryotaro eventually married and had two daughters. He lost his wife shortly after the birth of their second daughter, Hiroto's mother. Ryotaro supported his family by running a local store.

177

When the Pacific War began, he was drafted and served as a crewman on a transport ship. His ship was in Tokyo Bay during the Doolittle Raid on April 18, 1945.

The family resided in Hiroshima, and their house was located near the foot of Mount Hijiyama, close to the Hiroden Hijiyama Train Line. On August 6, 1945, when the United States dropped the atomic bomb on Hiroshima City, Ryotaro had the day off and was at home. Hiroto's aunt, Susume, was a student at the time, and she too was at home. Fortunately, they both managed to avoid being injured when their home was burned down. Years later, just before her death, Susume told Hiroto that she had seen people who were badly burned with their skin hanging down.

Ryotaro and Susume lived in a bomb shelter for approximately one month after the bombing. Subsequently, they were certified as hibakusha and returned to Niimi City.

The Atomic Bomb Survivors Relief Law classifies hibakusha into one or more of the following categories: (1) people who were within a few kilometers of the hypocenters of the bombs, (2) people who were within two kilometers of the hypocenters within two weeks of the bombs, (3) people who were exposed to radiation from the fallout, and (4) people who were not yet born but were carried by pregnant women in any of the previous categories. Overall, the Japanese government has certified approximately 650,000 as hibakusha. Of the 174,080 hibakusha still alive as of March 31, 2016, the government recognizes one percent as having illnesses caused by radiation exposure. The hibakusha are entitled to receive government support, a certain amount of money given to them each month. The one percent recognized as having bomb-related diseases also receive a special medical allowance.

Ryotaro and Susume had a tendency to get sick often after returning from Hiroshima. Although they were compensated by the government, the compensation was not enough to cover the costs of their medical care. Fortunately, since Susume worked at the town office, the family had the financial means to adequately handle their medical expenses. Hiroto's grandfather and aunt passed away without saying too much about the bombing of Hiroshima. Ryotaro passed away from cancer in July of 1984. Susume passed away in October of 2008 due to a stroke. She had never been married.

A year after the passing of his aunt, Hiroto attended a ceremony held at the Hiroshima Peace Memorial Park as a representative of Okayama prefecture.

The names of the deceased hibakusha are memorialized in Hiroshima and Nagasaki. The list is updated annually on the anniversaries of the bombings.

Hiroto's uncle, Seiji Sakamoto, was drafted into the Japanese Imperial Army and served in Manchuria. He was assigned to reconnaissance duties and positioned near the Soviet border. When Russia invaded Manchuria on August 9, 1945, he was captured and sent to Siberia as a prisoner of war. He had reached the rank of sergeant at that time, and his rank earned him better treatment at the POW camp, according to Hiroto.

Of the total number of Japanese POWs interned in Siberian and Mongolian camps, it is said that approximately ten percent (60,000) died from hard labor, illness, and starvation. The majority of the deaths occurred during the winter of 1945–46. The soldiers, dressed only in their military uniforms, were forced to cut trees, toiled in construction work, and engaged in coal mining in

179

temperatures hovering around -40C.

The Japanese POWs in Siberia refused to call themselves prisoners of war. Rather, they referred to themselves as *Yokuryusha*, or detainees. This was a reflection of the Japanese Imperial Army's disdain for being captured. The Japanese soldiers were indoctrinated to choose death over being captured. Also, they contended that they were not captured in battle, but like Japanese forces elsewhere, they laid down their arms to obey the Emperor's order following the August 15, 1945 broadcast announcing Japan's surrender.

The repatriation of Japanese POWs began in 1946. Seiji returned to Niimi City in 1947. On January 22, 1992, Russia formally issued certificates to former Japanese POWs for their forced labor in Siberia. These certificates were the first step enabling the former Japanese detainees to seek compensation for their forced labor after World War II.

Unfortunately, the Soviets only went as far as issuing a formal apology for the inhumane treatment of Japanese POWs. The government never financially compensated the former detainees, pointing to the provisions set forth in the October 9, 1956 Joint Declaration signed by the Soviet and Japanese governments, in which both sides agreed to waive all World War II reparations claims.

The former detainees filed a long-running lawsuit alleging that the Japanese government had abandoned and neglected them. While the lawsuit initially failed in the Japanese Supreme Court in 1997, the Japanese Diet eventually passed a bill calling for the compensation of all living survivors. Since the passage of the bill, approximately 69,000 survivors have applied for and received small payments ranging between ¥250,000 and ¥1.5 million each, depending on each person's length of internment. Hiroto's uncle was one of the detainees who has benefitted from the passage of the bill. He passed away in October of 2014, at the age of 93.

**Name:** Setsuko (Dorothy) Shinmoto
**Birthplace:** Watsonville, California

Dorothy Shinmoto was only six years old when a government agent knocked on the door and ordered her family to pack up their belongings and report to the Salinas Assembly Center. President Franklin D. Roosevelt had signed Executive Order 9066 on February 19, 1942, clearing the way for the internment of Japanese Americans residing on the West Coast.

The family was not given very much time to gather their personal belongings prior to reporting to the Salinas Assembly Center, one of fifteen temporary detention centers operated by the Wartime Civil Control Administration. Possessions they could not take with them were either stored or discarded.

The Salinas Center was in operation from April 27 to July 4, 1942. It was comprised of 165 buildings with barracks located north and east of the racetrack. During the height of its operation, the camp's population reached 3,608. The facilities were originally designed to hold a maximum of 3,594 individuals. Japanese Americans who reported to this center were later transferred to either the Poston or the Tule Lake internment camps.

Dorothy's family was sent to the Poston War Relocation Center in Arizona. Poston was actually comprised of three separate camps, Poston I, II and III, situated approximately three miles apart from each other along what is now Mohave Road. It was the most populous camp until Tule Lake was turned into a segregation facility. Tule Lake was originally constructed as an internment camp; however, following the 1943 administration of the loyalty questionnaire, internees who refused to give unqualified "yes" responses were segregated at Tule Lake and labeled as disloyal.

182

Poston was built on the Colorado River Indian Reservation, and Dorothy recalls seeing Native Americans after disembarking from the train. Her only knowledge of Native Americans came from Hollywood's portrayal, and she recalls being frightened and holding on to father's leg.

Dorothy was one of five children. Her father was a strawberry farmer who worked for Driscoll's, a company founded in 1904 by Joseph Reiter and Richard Driscoll.

Dorothy and her family were housed in Block 39, Barrack 15, Camp #1, which she still clearly recalls today at age 82. They were given one room and a single bed for each member of the family. Each barrack was divided into four sections, with only one section allocated to an entire household. There were no walls separating the individual living spaces; therefore, the residents hung sheets and blankets for privacy. Bathrooms and showers were communal and located at some distance away from the barracks.

The internees ate their meals in a large mess hall, where they were provided with three meals per day. The menu consisted of Japanese American style meals prepared and served by other internees at the camp. The government only allotted about 40 cents per meal and made from whatever was cheapest and easiest to get; the food was inedible to most of the internees. The internees reportedly went on strike after they were served liver for several weeks.

Poston had agricultural fields within a fenced-in area where internees grew vegetables for the camp and commercial consumption, and they also raised chickens and hogs. By the end of the second year of operation, the internees produced 85 percent of the vegetables they consumed. Over 1,400 acres of vegetables and 800 acres of field crops were under cultivation.

The camp had two schools. The elementary school was housed in one of the residential blocks. The high school was located in a large open space just below the administrative area, and included an office, a library, an auditorium, and eight classroom buildings, all made of adobe.

Dorothy recalls that classes were taught by American teachers. The quality of education was lacking due to the shortage of materials and qualified teachers. The only qualification for a camp teacher was the completion of a college degree. In addition to the required subjects, children participated in singing, dancing, storytelling, drawing, and crafts. Dorothy's teacher could not pronounce her Japanese name, Setsuko; therefore, she was given an American name. The same applied for sister, Sakaye, who was named Elaine.

The children were told about Pearl Harbor and the bombings of Hiroshima and Nagasaki, but they were different worlds to them. The children really didn't understand the significance of these events. Dorothy saw people crying after the news was disclosed and asked her mother what was happening. Her mother responded that they were at war and there was nothing they could do. Dorothy's mother advised her to do her best to get along and survive the ordeal.

When not attending classes or focusing on their homework, the interned children played games to pass the time. Dorothy smiled as she recalls playing with paper dolls.

The internees at Poston were allowed to work both inside and outside the camp. Inside, they did a variety of jobs and were paid from $12 to $19 a month. They could work as farm laborers outside the camp, and college students were allowed to leave to finish their education. Dorothy's father had the job of cleaning the bathrooms in the camp. He would start work at 4:00 a.m. before the camp residents woke up. Her mother helped out at the mess hall, and the kids also pitched in.

In the spring of 1944, Executive Order 9066 was lifted and the internees were finally allowed to return home. By November 28, 1945, the last internees had left Poston. Some Japanese repatriated and moved back to Japan, but most chose to stay in the United States. Dorothy's family was given money to purchase bus tickets and they settled in Madrone, California. Her father went back to work for Driscoll Strawberry Associates. Following World War II, Driscoll's recruited former Japanese American internees to become sharecroppers for the company.

The returning families lived in tents until Driscoll Strawberry Associates constructed homes for them. Dorothy recalls that 15 houses were constructed. The house where she and her family lived had an old-fashioned Japanese bath (*ofuro*) and it was her job to prepare the bath for her family.

When Dorothy and her siblings returned home from school, they helped to pick strawberries until 6:00 p.m.. From 9:00 p.m. to 10:00 p.m., the children concentrated on their homework. The families who worked for Driscoll were given Saturdays off, which was typically devoted to housework and laundry. They all worked very hard.

Dorothy's husband, Minoru Shinmoto, was also interned during World War II. Born in Upland, California on June 30, 1925, he was one of five children born to Tsunetaro and Haruyo Shinmoto from

185

Hiroshima, Japan. Minoru and his family were interned at the Gila Relocation Camp in Rivers, Arizona.

In 1944, Minoru was drafted into the United States Army, and he completed his basic training at Fort McClellan in Alabama. After his basic training, he was recruited by the Military Intelligence Service (MIS) in Fort Snelling, Minnesota. The MIS was a World War II US military unit comprised of nisei (second generation Japanese Americans) who were trained as linguists. Graduates of the MIS Language School (MISLS) were assigned to other military units to provide translation, interpretation, and interrogation services. Minoru's schooling was terminated after only eight months when the war ended.

He was sent to Fukuoka, Japan as part of the occupation forces and served in the Civil Censorship Detachment. He later led a team of ten MIS operatives who interrogated repatriates from Manchuria. The interrogations took place at the Hario Repatriation Center located in Sasebo, Nagasaki. He was discharged in November of 1946.

The MIS's record was kept secret for 30 years after the war. General Charles Willoughby, a major general in the United States Army who served as General Douglas MacArthur's chief of intelligence, stated that the MIS shortened the war by two years and saved over a million American and Japanese lives.

Racial prejudice was common when the former internees returned home. Dorothy recalls being teased and called names such as "dirty Jap." Despite the harassment, she and others around her never fought back. They maintained their dignity as best they could and continued to rebuild their lives.

When asked about her overall impression about being interned, Dorothy believes that her parents might have had views different than her own; however, as a kid, she recalls being carefree, as kids tend to be, even during such difficult times.

**Name:** Fusako (Uyemura) Takahashi
**Birthplace:** Stockton, California

When the Uyemura family received their orders to evacuate their home in Cortez, California, Fusako was just 14 years old and a freshman in high school. Cortez was a small Japanese farming community founded in 1919 by Kyutaro Abiko, a Japanese newspaper editor, businessman, and prominent leader in the Japanese American community. In addition to founding the Japanese community in Cortez, Abiko also founded the Yamato Colony in Livingston in 1907, and another Japanese community at Cressey. Born in Niigata prefecture, Abiko came to the United States as a student in 1885. After achieving success as a businessman, he began his personal mission to aid his fellow Japanese in settling in America.

Fusako's parents were issei from Kyushu, Japan. All the children, with the exception of then 21-year-old Tomiko Uyemura, were born in California. The youngest of the children, a boy named Koichi, was only a year old when the family was interned.

Fusako's family of nine were ordered to report to the Merced Assembly Center located on the Merced Fairgrounds. There were more than 4,000 residents of Japanese ancestry incarcerated at the Merced Assembly Center. They came from the central California communities of Merced, Livingston, Turlock, Cortez, Sebastopol, Yuba City, Yolo, Walnut Grove, Colusa, Winters, Modesto, Woodland, Santa Rosa, Chico, Marin, Napa, and Courtland. Fusako recalls that they were each allowed to bring one small suitcase with them, and they had to pack their own plate, cutlery, and cup.

There were 200 buildings constructed at the Merced Assembly

Center and most were located south of the fairgrounds. The barracks measured 20 feet by 100 feet. Fusako remembers that the bathroom facilities were quite terrible; they had no privacy, which was very hard to accept, especially for a young teenage girl. Since they were a family of nine, they received two "rooms" in the barracks. The Uyemuras spent three months at the assembly center before being transferred to Camp Amache, whose formal name was The Granada War Relocation Center.

Fusako remembers that the facilities at Camp Amache were a little better, since at least there were partitions between the toilets with no door. The bathrooms were communal and located in the middle of the block. There were twelve barracks in each block.

Camp Amache opened on August 27, 1942 and reached its peak population of 7,318 persons by February 1943. It was considered to be the smallest of the War Relocation Authority (WRA) camps. Amache was surrounded by barbed wire fencing with eight towers located all around the camp. The residential area was situated atop a low hill, which prevented flooding, an issue that frequently plagued other WRA camps. Unfortunately, this semi-arid, high plains country was prone to high winds and severe dust storms. Fusako recollects that the barracks were so crudely built that it was common to wake up after a dust storm and find their beds and faces covered with sand. She said it was particularly bad in the mess halls when they were trying to eat. The sand would cover the tables and get into their food.

Fusako's two older sisters, Tomiko and Nuiko, worked as waitresses in the mess hall, for which they were paid $16 a month. Fusako also worked after school. She was a part-time tray girl in the hospital. She was paid $8 per month for preparing the trays of food for the patients.

189

Children were able to attend school at the camp. Amache High School was completed in June of 1943, but plans to construct two additional schools for elementary and junior high students were abandoned amid protests by the residents of Granada and other nearby communities. The problem was that the area was still recovering from the Depression of the 1930s and citizens argued that their tax dollars should not go to support Japanese American students.

Fusako recalls that the education system was accredited and rather good. Her teachers, mostly Caucasians, were very dedicated and some of them stayed in the camp. Fusako graduated from high school in May of 1945. There was a graduation ceremony where she received her diploma. She had applied for scholarships to attend college and was prepared to go; however, her parents wanted her to stay with them and help out financially.

The camp established a silkscreen shop in 1943. It employed forty-five staff members, who were involved in creating training materials and produced over 250,000 color posters for the United States Navy. The shop also produced calendars, event programs, and other personal use items for the camp's residents. Fusako mentioned that they had a yearbook called the *Onlooker* which was also printed in the silkscreen shop.

By mid-1943, the Project Director at Camp Amache, James G. Lindley, allowed the internees to take day trips to the town of Granada, located within walking distance of the camp. Internees were also allowed to leave the camp for work as long as the jobs were not on the West Coast.

Fusako went shopping in Granada and Lamar, seventeen miles

away. She and others were transported to town in Army trucks driven by camp personnel. No guards accompanied them, but there was a roll call afterward to make sure everyone made it back to camp. The businesses and shop owners were friendly and happy to have the extra sales from the camp residents.

For recreation, the camp residents formed baseball teams. They also held talent shows, and films were shown in the mess hall once a week. There was plenty to do for fun, and to pass the time; however, Fusako remembers that it was a very difficult time for her parents. They were in a financial bind, unable to earn any real money for over three years, and had a large family to support.

The family left the camp in the summer of 1945. They were given $25 per person and had nothing else, such as furniture, household goods, etc. When they evacuated their personal belongings were stored in their Japanese church, but the church was later burglarized and they lost everything.

The Uyemuras settled in Alamosa, Colorado where Fusako's uncle had a farm. They remained there for a year and then returned to California, settling in San Francisco. Fusako will be 91 years old in May of 2018. To this day, she is still amazed at how well her family endured such a horrific existence during the war. Fortunately, they were able to rebuild their lives and have all managed to do well.

# POSTSCRIPT

Although Japan officially surrendered on August 15, 1945, marking the end of the Pacific War, Japanese forces were driven to battle the invading Soviet forces between August 18 and September 1, 1945 during what became known as the Invasion of the Kuril Islands.

The Kuril Islands are a chain of 56 islands in the Russian Far East, located directly to the north of Japan and east of Sakhalin Island. The *Ainu*, the indigenous people of Japan, were early inhabitants of the islands. Japan first took nominal control of the islands during the Edo period (1603–1868).

During the Tehran and Yalta Conferences in 1943 and 1945 respectively, Soviet leader Joseph Stalin had secretly reached an agreement with the Allies to declare war on Japan. As a result, the United States began aiding the Soviets by transferring ships and aircraft to the Soviet armed forces. In the spring and summer of 1945, the United States transferred 149 ships and aircraft, mostly escort vessels, landing craft, and minesweepers to the Soviet Navy in a covert operation known as Project Hula.

On April 5, 1945, the Soviet Union informed Japan that the Soviet-Japanese Neutrality Pact of 1941 would not be renewed. On August 9, 1945, just six months short of the natural expiration of the neutrality pact and the day when the United States dropped an atomic bomb over Nagasaki, the Soviet Union officially declared war on Japan. In the days that ensued, Soviet troops marched into Manchuria, the Japanese prefecture of Karafuto (South Sakhalin), and the northern half of Korea, in what became known as the Manchurian Strategic Offensive. The Japanese northernmost island of Hokkaido was initially included in the invasion plans, but since Japan had surrendered, paving the way for the Allied Occupation, the Soviet forces could not mount their invasion as planned.

During the occupation, however, the Soviet Union repeatedly demanded that Hokkaido be administered by Soviet forces independent of the Supreme Commander of Allied Powers. General Douglas MacArthur was sternly opposed to the idea and threatened the Soviets with military action should they set foot on the island.

There were over 400,000 people living in Karafuto at the time. The majority of these residents were of Japanese or Korean extraction. Japan began evacuating people from Karafuto and the Kuriles to Hokkaido just before the invasion began. Approximately 6,000 civilians had been evacuated from the area when the Soviet forces began a fierce naval bombardment and artillery strikes against the civilians who were still awaiting evacuation. On August 10, nearly 1,000 civilians were killed by machine-gun fire.

Despite this, there were twelve telephone operators in Karafuto who decided to stay behind and maintain contact with mainland Japan. By August 23, the Japanese forces had agreed to a ceasefire. Upon learning of Japan's surrender and fearing that they would be raped by the Soviet troops, nine of the twelve operators committed suicide by ingesting cyanide capsules. Three of the operators were saved by the intervention of their male colleagues.

Karafuto prefecture was formally abolished as a legal entity on June 1, 1949. Japan renounced its rights to Sakhalin in 1951 with the signing of the Treaty of San Francisco, but did not formally acknowledge Russian sovereignty over the island. To date, no final peace treaty has been signed between Japan and Russia and the status of the neighboring Kuril Islands remains disputed.

195

Please turn the page for an excerpt from
**A BLOGGER'S GUIDE TO JAPAN**
Available on Amazon.com
Kindle
CreateSpace: createspace.com/6595032

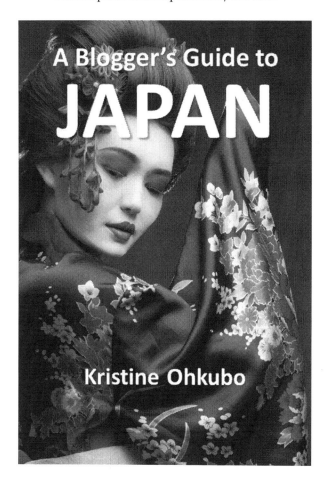

ISBN-10: 1539033112
ISBN-13: 978-1539033110

# Introduction

For many, the island country of Japan is a far distant place characterized by temples, shrines, kabuki, Noh, tea ceremonies, ikebana, kimonos, geisha, and samurai. They often dream about visiting this alluring nation, but few actually have an opportunity to do so.

However, for those who do travel to Japan, it becomes a destination that they visit over and over again. As a matter of fact, Japan received a record number 12 million visitors in 2014 and is seeking to increase tourism up to 20 million visitors by 2020. With the Olympic Games scheduled to take place in Tokyo in 2020, that number does not appear far-fetched.

I had the pleasure of traveling to Japan on several occasions, fell in love with the country, and vowed to return many times. I approached each visit with wide-eyed enthusiasm, immersing myself in the local culture and learning about the history and traditions of this magnificent place that once I only dreamed about. I fell in love with Japan and its people and wanted to share my experiences with others so that they too would carve out an opportunity to someday travel there. I found that the easiest way to reach people in this age of technology and social media was by creating a blog. Thus, Traveldreamscapes was born.

I published numerous blog posts and photos gathered from my travels, which was received with so much enthusiasm by my readers that several asked me whether I had intentions of writing a book about my travels to Japan. At first, the idea seemed daunting but the more I thought about it, the more I gravitated toward the notion.

Certainly, there are countless travel books about Japan but I wondered how many were actually written from a travel blogger's perspective. You will find that this book offers a different approach to introducing both new and seasoned travelers to Japan. I will give you the history and background of each place to help you develop a greater appreciation for the sites you visit. Not only will you learn about the popular destinations for tourists but you will also discover attractions off the beaten path. I will uncover festivals and traditions unique to each area and introduce you to local cuisines.

One of the best ways to immerse yourself in a culture is to sample its diverse cuisine. While traveling in Japan today, you will find many western chain restaurants as well as western-style eateries to choose among. Rather than settling for the familiar places, select a traditional restaurant frequented by the locals and sample some of Japan's regional cooking.

Japanese cuisine has a vast array of local specialties known as kyodo ryori (郷土料理). These dishes are typically prepared using local ingredients and traditional recipes. Although many local ingredients are available nationwide these days and it is not uncommon to find regional dishes throughout Japan, you can still find true kyodo ryori to fulfill your adventures in gastronomy. After all, your travels should be an adventure where you actively engage in the traditions and offerings of a country rather than just observing as a bystander.

The book is organized by region/prefecture so regardless of whether you are traveling for a week, a month or several months, you can use this book not only to plan your travels but also to explore further once you are there. Where available, the web page address, physical address, and travel tips will enable you to obtain current, detailed information for each venue.

It is my hope that this guide to Japan will awaken your curiosity about this beautiful country and encourage you to explore it on your own.  To quote J.R.R. Tolkien, "Little by little, one travels far."

Wishing you happy and safe journeys to Japan!

# Hokkaido Region
## Introduction to Hokkaido (北海道)

Formerly known as Ezochi, Hokkaido is located in the northernmost region of Japan and is the second largest island next to Honshu, the main island. It represents 22 percent of Japan's total land mass, yet it is home to only five percent of the country's total population.

The area was exclusively inhabited by the Ainu (Japan's native people) until the Edo era (1603-1868) when mainlanders began moving into the southwest region of the province.

During the Meiji era (1868-1912), a period when Japan underwent a major transformation and emerged as the modern nation we know today, the Ezochi Province became known as Hokkaido (where "Hokkai (北海)" means north sea and "do (道)" denotes its prefectural status).

Travelers need to be aware that the region's weather can be rather harsh in the winter with heavy snowfalls and below zero temperatures. During the summer, however, Hokkaido is a welcome retreat from the hot and humid temperatures that are common throughout the rest of the country.

The largest city and the capital of Hokkaido is Sapporo which hosted the Olympic Winter Games in 1972 and is home to the Sapporo Yuki Matsuri (Sapporo Snow Festival), an annual festival held during February. The city is also where the Sapporo Brewery originated during the Meiji period.

Hokkaido's numerous national parks are a major draw for many visitors. Other notable attractions include flower gardens, hot springs, and some of the best powder skiing opportunities available in Japan.

The regional dishes that characterize Hokkaido include: Genghis Khan (barbecued lamb and vegetables), ishikari nabe (a stewed dish consisting of salmon and vegetables in a miso based broth), ruibe (an Ainu dish of sliced, frozen raw salmon served with soy sauce and water peppers), sanpei jiru (a winter miso soup made with salmon, daikon radish, carrots, potatoes and onions), chanchan yaki (a miso grilled salmon with beansprouts and other vegetables, a specialty in fishing villages), Hokkaido ramen (especially Sapporo ramen) and ika somen (squid sliced into very thin noodle-like strips and eaten with dipping sauce).

Of course, these are the more common regional dishes associated with Hokkaido. Hokkaido has 14 sub-prefectures (支庁/ shicho) and, as a result, you can probably delve deeper into the region's specific cuisine by visiting each individual shicho.

Hokkaido is connected to Honshu via the Seikan Tunnel Underwater Railway, part of the Kaikyo Line portion of the Hokkaido Railway Company's (JR Hokkaido) Tsugaru-Kaikyo Line.

The New Chitose Airport (http://www.new-chitose-airport.jp/en/ ) is the largest airport in Hokkaido serving the Sapporo metropolitan area. Opened in 1991, it is one of the busiest airports in Japan and serves the world's most traveled air route between Tokyo and Sapporo.

# PHOTO CREDITS

1. Hand drawn map of Japanese Empire in late 1941 - early 1942. The beginning of the Pacific War. Original Illustration: Keith Tarrier / Shutterstock.com
2. Japanese Imperial Army in Manchuria: Hiroto Sakamoto
3. Kempeitai Headquarters in Nanking, China: Masayuki Ohkubo
4. Kempeitai Officer: Masayuki Ohkubo
5. Explosion of the USS Shaw (Pearl Harbor, Dec. 7, 1941): Everett Historical / Shutterstock.com
6. Manzanar Relocation Center, Photograph by Ansel Adams: Everett Historical /Shutterstock.com
7. Interned Japanese American, Sumiko Shigematsu, Photograph by Ansel Adams: Everett Historical / Shutterstock.com
8. Japanese American veteran, dressed in his WWI uniform, reports for his WWII internment. Photo by Dorothea Lange: Everett Historical / Shutterstock.com
9. Injured female survivor of Nagasaki atomic bombing. Sept. 1945: Everett Historical/ Shutterstock.com
10. World War II atomic bombing aftermath in suburb four miles outside of center of Nagasaki, Japan: Everett Historical/ Shutterstock.com
11. Tokyo's shanty town, where post-World War II homeless Japanese have set up housekeeping in small huts amid the ruins from wartime bombing. September 26, 1945: Everett Historical / Shutterstock.com
12. Food stall in post-World War II Tokyo: Everett Historical/ Shutterstock.com
13. Homeless Japanese in Tokyo: Everett Historical/ Shutterstock.com
14. Hiroshima Prisoner of War Sub-Camp No. 4 Memorial in Onomichi: Shotaro Aoyama
15. Seki Hanuda: Masayuki Ohkubo
16. Betty Hasegawa: Aylen Hasegawa
17. Loyalty Questionnaire: Aylen Hasegawa

# BIBLIOGRAPHY

*"17th Division (Imperial Japanese Army)." Wikipedia. Accessed July 6, 2017.*
*https://en.wikipedia.org/wiki/17th_Division_(Imperial_Japanese_Army).*

*"1964 Summer Olympics." Wikipedia. March 2, 2017.*
*https://en.wikipedia.org/wiki/1964_Summer_Olympics.*

*Adachi, Stephanie. E-mail interview by author. April 12, 2017.*

*Advantage, Military. Iwo Jima: A Remembrance. Accessed December 8, 2016.*
*http://www.military.com/NewContent/0,13190,NI_Iwo_Jima2,00.html.*

*"Air raids on Japan." Wikipedia. December 22, 2016. Accessed September 28, 2017. https://en.wikipedia.org/wiki/Air_raids_on_Japan.*

*Aldrich, Richard J. The faraway war: personal diaries of the Second World War in Asia and the Pacific. London: Transworld Digital, 2014.*

*"Atomic bombings of Hiroshima and Nagasaki." Wikipedia. Accessed December 12, 2016.*
*https://en.wikipedia.org/wiki/Atomic_bombings_of_Hiroshima_and_Nagasaki.*

*"Attack on Pearl Harbor." Wikipedia. Accessed December 12, 2016.*
*https://en.wikipedia.org/wiki/Attack_on_Pearl_Harbor.*

*Barford, Vanessa. "The Japanese women who married the enemy." BBC News. August 16, 2015. Accessed January 6, 2017.*
*http://www.bbc.com/news/magazine-33857059.*

*"Battle of Iwo Jima." In WWII in HD. History Channel. December 4, 2016.*

*"Battle of Iwo Jima." Wikipedia. Accessed December 8, 2016.*
*https://en.wikipedia.org/wiki/Battle_of_Iwo_Jima.*

"Battle of Okinawa." In WWII in HD. History Channel. December 4, 2016.

"Battle of Okinawa." Wikipedia. Accessed December 8, 2016. https://en.wikipedia.org/wiki/Battle_of_Okinawa.

"Battle of Okinawa: The Bloodiest Battle of the Pacific War." HistoryNet. Accessed December 8, 2016. http://www.historynet.com/battle-of-okinawa-the-bloodiest-battle-of-the-pacific-war.htm.

"Bombing of Nagoya in World War II." Wikipedia. Accessed December 8, 2016. https://en.wikipedia.org/wiki/Bombing_of_Nagoya_in_World_War_II.

"Bushido." Wikipedia. Accessed December 14, 2016. https://en.wikipedia.org/wiki/Bushido.

Chappell, Bill. "It's Fred Korematsu Day: Celebrating A Foe Of U.S. Internment Camps." NPR. Accessed January 31, 2017. http://www.npr.org/sections/thetwo-way/2017/01/30/512488821/its-fred-korematsu-day-celebrating-a-foe-of-u-s-internment-camps?utm_source=facebook.com&utm_medium=social&utm_campaign=npr&utm_term=nprnews&utm_content=20170130.

Chen, C. Peter. "Bombing of Tokyo and Other Cities." WW2DB. Accessed July 6,, 2017. http://ww2db.com/battle_spec.php?battle_id=217.

"Civilians on Okinawa." American Experience. Accessed December 8, 2016. http://www.pbs.org/wgbh/americanexperience/features/general-article/pacific-civilians-okinawa/.

Commodore Perry and Japan (1853-1854) | Asia for Educators | Columbia University. Accessed December 12, 1016. http://afe.easia.columbia.edu/special/japan_1750_perry.htm.

"Communist Revolution of China." Wikipedia. Accessed December 12, 2016. https://en.wikipedia.org/wiki/Communist_Revolution_of_China.

"Containment." *Wikipedia.* Accessed December 12, 1016. https://en.wikipedia.org/wiki/Containment.

Contributor, Quora. "How Did the U.S. Break Japanese Military Codes Before the Battle of Midway?" *Slate Magazine.* November 20, 2013. Accessed March 8, 2017. http://www.slate.com/blogs/quora/2013/11/20/u_s_in_world_war_ii_ho w_the_navy_broke_japanese_codes_before_midway.html.

Corrigan, Kelly. "Verdugo Hills Golf Course will close and a proposal to build a gated community is on the table." *Los Angeles Times.* November 22, 2016. Accessed August 14, 2017. http://www.latimes.com/socal/glendale-news-press/news/tn-gnp-me-golf-course-20161122-story.html.

Documentary on Japanese 'war brides' is gaining steam." *The Japan Times.* Accessed January 6, 2017. http://www.japantimes.co.jp/culture/2015/04/08/films/documentary-japanese-war-brides-gaining-steam/#.WHAm333yQkQ.

Editor, Tim Sharp Reference. "International Space Station: Facts, History & Tracking." *Space.com.* Accessed February 28, 2017. http://www.space.com/16748-international-space-station.html.

"Elizabeth Saunders Home." *Wikipedia.* Accessed May 17, 2017. https://en.wikipedia.org/wiki/Elizabeth_Saunders_Home.

"Emperor of Japan." *Wikipedia.* Accessed December 14, 2016. https://en.wikipedia.org/wiki/Emperor_of_Japan.

"Enigma machine." *Wikipedia.* Accessed December 14, ,2016. https://en.wikipedia.org/wiki/Enigma_machine.

"Estelle Ishigo." *Estelle Ishigo | Densho Encyclopedia.* Accessed March 27, 2017. http://encyclopedia.densho.org/Estelle%20Ishigo/.

"Estelle Peck Ishigo." *Wikipedia.* Accessed March 27, 2017. https://en.wikipedia.org/wiki/Estelle_Peck_Ishigo.

Falgout, Suzanne, and Linda Nishigaya. *Breaking the silence: lessons of democracy and social justice from the World War II Honouliuli Internment and POW Camp in Hawaii.* Honolulu: Department of Sociology, University of Hawaii at Mānoa, 2014.

*FBI Raids: World War II & Roundup | Exploring JAI.* Accessed March 27, 2017. http://caamedia.org/jainternment/ww2/fbi.html.

"FDR signs Neutrality Act." *History.com.* Accessed February 28, 2017. http://www.history.com/this-day-in-history/fdr-signs-neutrality-act.

"FDR's Pearl Harbor Bait." *The Future of Freedom Foundation.* Accessed February 28, 2017. http://www.fff.org/2016/12/07/fdrs-pearl-harbor-bait/.

Fenton, Ben. "American troops 'murdered Japanese PoWs'." *The Telegraph.* August 06, 2005. Accessed July 11, 2017. http://www.telegraph.co.uk/news/worldnews/asia/japan/1495651/American-troops-murdered-Japanese-PoWs.html.

"Financing peacekeeping. United Nations Peacekeeping." *United Nations.* Accessed March 2, 2017. http://www.un.org/en/peacekeeping/operations/financing.shtml.

"Firebombing of Tokyo." *History.com.* Accessed December 12, 2016. http://www.history.com/this-day-in-history/firebombing-of-tokyo.

"First kamikaze attack of the war begins." *History.com.* Accessed March 2, 2017. http://www.history.com/this-day-in-history/first-kamikaze-attack-of-the-war-begins.

"Fred Korematsu." *Wikipedia.* Accessed January 31, 2017. https://en.wikipedia.org/wiki/Fred_Korematsu.

"Fukuryu." *Wikipedia.* Accessed March 1, 2017. https://en.wikipedia.org/wiki/Fukuryu.

"GENERAL ANAMI KORECHIKA." Who's Who and What'd They Do? . Accessed December 14, 2016. http://www.doug-long.com/anami.htm.

"Gila River War Relocation Center." Wikipedia. Accessed December 12, 2016. https://en.wikipedia.org/wiki/Gila_River_War_Relocation_Center.

Glines, C.V."The Bomb That Ended the War." HistoryNet. Accessed January 17, 2017. http://www.historynet.com/world-war-ii-second-atomic-bomb-that-ended-the-war.htm.

Go For Broke National Education Center - Preserving the Legacy of the Japanese American Veterans of World War II. Accessed January 26, 2017. http://www.goforbroke.org/learn/history/military_units/442nd.php.

"Gordon Hirabayashi." Gordon Hirabayashi | Densho Encyclopedia. Accessed December 12, 2016. http://encyclopedia.densho.org/Gordon_Hirabayashi/.

"Granada Relocation Center." Wikipedia. Accessed December 12, 2016. https://en.wikipedia.org/wiki/Granada_Relocation_Center.

Grier, Peter. "Pearl Harbor attack: Who was really to blame?" The Christian Science Monitor. December 10, 2009. Accessed December 6, 2016. http://www.csmonitor.com/USA/2009/1210/p02s04-usgn.html.

Hamilton, Walter Stuart. Children of the Occupation: Japan's Untold Story. New Brunswick: NewSouth.

Hanuda, Seki. Interview by author. February 5, 2017.

Hasegawa, Aylen. E-mail interview by author. August 14, 2017.

Hasegawa, Curt. E-mail interview by author. March 17, 2017.

211

Herald, The Hawaii. "University Of Hawai'i Honors WWII's Varsity Victory Volunteers." *The Hawaii Herald*. May 11, 2015. Accessed August 2, 2017. http://thehawaiiherald.com/2015/05/university-of-hawaii-honors-wwiis-varsity-victory-volunteers/.

"Hibakusha." *Wikipedia*. Accessed July 5, 2017. https://en.wikipedia.org/wiki/Hibakusha.

Hickman, Kennedy. "The Battle of Iwo Jima: A Costly Victory." *ThoughtCo*. Accessed December 8, 2016. http://militaryhistory.about.com/od/worldwarii/p/battle-of-iwo-jima.htm.

Hiroshima and Nagasaki Death Toll. Accessed December 14, 2016. http://www.aasc.ucla.edu/cab/200708230009.html.

"Hiroshima Maidens." *Wikipedia.*. Accessed February 6, 2017. https://en.wikipedia.org/wiki/Hiroshima_Maidens.

Hiroshima Returning to Life. Accessed May 17, 2017. http://www.pcf.city.hiroshima.jp/kids/KPSH_E/hiroshima_e/sadako_e/subcontents_e/12yomigaeru_1_e.html.

History.com Staff. "Battle of Iwo Jima." *History.com*. 2009. Accessed December 8, 2016. http://www.history.com/topics/world-war-ii/battle-of-iwo-jima.

"How Did the Japanese Draft Citizens in World War II?" *HistoryNet*. Accessed January 11, 2017. http://www.historynet.com/how-did-the-japanese-draft-citizens-in-world-war-ii.htm.

"Humanity Declaration." *Wikipedia*. Accessed February 28, 2017. https://en.wikipedia.org/wiki/Humanity_Declaration.

"HWS: Miki Sawada." *Hobart and William Smith Colleges*. Accessed May 17, 2017. http://www.hws.edu/about/blackwell/sawada.aspx.

Imperial Rescript. Accessed February 28, 2017. http://home.wlu.edu/~lubint/Rel103/ImpRescript46.html.

"Internment of Japanese & Japanese Americans in Hawaii: Home." *LibGuides.* Accessed July 21, 2017. http://guides.library.manoa.hawaii.edu/Hawaii_internment.

"Internment of Japanese Americans." *Wikipedia.* Accessed December 13, 2016. https://en.wikipedia.org/wiki/Internment_of_Japanese_Americans.

"Invasion of the Kuril Islands." *Wikipedia.* Accessed August 15, 2017. https://en.wikipedia.org/wiki/Invasion_of_the_Kuril_Islands.

"Japan WW2 soldier who refused to surrender Hiroo Onoda dies." *BBC News.* January 17, 2014. Accessed March 2, 2017. http://www.bbc.com/news/world-asia-25772192.

"Japanese economic miracle." *Wikipedia.* Accessed January 5, 2017. https://en.wikipedia.org/wiki/Japanese_economic_miracle.

*Japanese economic takeoff after 1945.* Accessed January 5, 2017. http://www.iun.edu/~hisdcl/h207_2002/jecontakeoff.htm.

"Japanese History/The American Occupation of Japan." *Japanese History/The American Occupation of Japan - Wikibooks, open books for an open world.* Accessed December 14, 2016. https://en.wikibooks.org/wiki/Japanese_History/The_American_Occupation_of_Japan.

"Japanese Instrument of Surrender." *Japanese Instrument of Surrender - Wikisource, the free online library.* Accessed December 14, 2016. https://en.wikisource.org/wiki/Japanese_Instrument_of_Surrender.

"Japanese Internment." *CBCnews.* Accessed February 28, 2017. http://www.cbc.ca/history/EPISCONTENTSE1EP14CH3PA3LE.html.

"Japanese naval codes." *Wikipedia.* Accessed January 5, 2017. https://en.wikipedia.org/wiki/Japanese_naval_codes#JN-25.

"Japanese-Canadian internment." *Wikipedia.* Accessed March 1, 2017. https://en.wikipedia.org/wiki/Japanese-Canadian_internment.

*"Japan's POWs interned in the Soviet Union still struggle for recognition."* The Australian. Accessed July 10, 2017. http://www.theaustralian.com.au/news/world/japans-pows-interned-in-the-soviet-union-still-struggle-for-recognition/news-story/b4f38933eabd4b0399417594c52a0f29.

*"Japan's role in the U.N."* The Japan Times. Accessed March 2, 2017. http://www.japantimes.co.jp/opinion/2006/12/21/editorials/japans-role-in-the-u-n/#.WLh2-n3ySUk.

*"Japan's space development."* Wikipedia. Accessed March 2, 2017. https://en.wikipedia.org/wiki/Japan%27s_space_development.

*"Japan–United States relations."* Wikipedia. Accessed January 24, 2017. https://en.wikipedia.org/wiki/Japan%E2%80%93United_States_relations.

*"JAXA."* Wikipedia. Accessed March 3, 2017. https://en.wikipedia.org/wiki/JAXA.

*"Jewel Voice Broadcast."* Wikipedia. Accessed March 2, 2017. https://en.wikipedia.org/wiki/Jewel_Voice_Broadcast.

Journal, The Asia Pacific. *"The Third Atomic Bomb."* The Asia-Pacific Journal: Japan Focus. Accessed January 17, 2017. http://apjjf.org/-Yoichi-Funabashi/1757/article.html.

*"Kaiten."* Wikipedia. Accessed February 1, 2017. https://en.wikipedia.org/wiki/Kaiten.

*"Kamikaze."* Wikipedia. Accessed February 1, 2017. https://en.wikipedia.org/wiki/Kamikaze.

*"Keiretsu."* Wikipedia. Accessed January 5, 2017. https://en.wikipedia.org/wiki/Keiretsu.

*"Kempeitai."* Wikipedia. Accessed January 13, 2017. https://en.wikipedia.org/wiki/Kempeitai.

"Kurogane. Accessed January 13, 2017.
http://www.3wheelers.com/kurogane.html.

"Kyūjō incident." Wikipedia. Accessed December 14, 2016.
https://en.wikipedia.org/wiki/Ky%C5%ABj%C5%8D_incident.

Lateline By North Asia correspondent Matthew Carney. "Horrors of the
past cast shadow on Okinawa's future battles." ABC News. July 20,
2015. Accessed December 12, 2016. http://www.abc.net.au/news/2015-
05-15/caught-in-the-middle-okinawa-still-battling-japan-and-
us/6473054.

"Lifetime – Fred T. Korematsu." Fred T. Korematsu Institute. Accessed
February 28, 2017. http://www.korematsuinstitute.org/fred-t-korematsu-
lifetime/.

List of Internment and Detention Camps. Accessed December 13, 2017.
http://www.momomedia.com/CLPEF/camps.html.

"Loyalty questionnaire." Loyalty questionnaire | Densho Encyclopedia.
Accessed February 22, 2017.
http://encyclopedia.densho.org/Loyalty_questionnaire/.

Lutton, Charles. "Pearl Harbor: Fifty Years of Controversy."
INSTITUTE FOR HISTORICAL REVIEW. Accessed December 6,
2016. http://www.ihr.org/jhr/v11/v11p431_Lutton.html.

"Magic (cryptography)." Wikipedia. Accessed December 7, 2016.
https://en.wikipedia.org/wiki/Magic_%28cryptography%29.

"Masanobu Tsuji." Wikipedia. Accessed January 4, 2017.
https://en.wikipedia.org/wiki/Masanobu_Tsuji.

"Merced (detention facility)." Merced (detention facility) | Densho
Encyclopedia. Accessed February 22, 2017.
http://encyclopedia.densho.org/Merced_%28detention_facility%29.

"Miki Sawada." Wikipedia. Accessed May 17, 2017.
https://en.wikipedia.org/wiki/Miki_Sawada.

Mills, Curtis. " *U.S. Returning Okinawa Land to Japan." US News and World Report. Accessed January 24, 2017.* http://www.usnews.com/news/world/articles/2016-12-21/us-returning-thousands-of-acres-on-okinawa-to-japan.

*"Minoru Yasui." Minoru Yasui | Densho Encyclopedia. Accessed May 17, 2017.* http://encyclopedia.densho.org/Minoru_Yasui/.

*"Mitsubishi." Wikipedia. Accessed May 17, 2017.* https://en.wikipedia.org/wiki/Mitsubishi.

*"Mitsuye Endo: The Woman Behind the Landmark Supreme Court Case." Densho: Japanese American Incarceration and Japanese Internment. March 24, 2016. Accessed March 27, 2017.* http://www.densho.org/mitsuye-endo/.

*Mullen, Jethro. "Japanese soldier who refused to surrender for decades dies at 91." CNN. January 3, 2014. Accessed September 28, 2017.* http://www.cnn.com/2014/01/17/world/asia/japan-philippines-ww2-soldier-dies.

*Nakanishi, Shinichi. E-mail interview by author. June 19, ,2017.*

*"Nanking Massacre." Wikipedia. Accessed January 13, 2017.* https://en.wikipedia.org/wiki/Nanking_Massacre.

*Narcisse, Evan. "The Raw Emotions That Will Make Mister Miracle One of the Best Comics You Read This Year." Io9. August 07, 2017. Accessed March 8, 2017.* http://io9.gizmodo.com/the-raw-emotions-that-will-make-mister-miracle-1-one-o-1797605846.

*"Naval Air Facility Atsugi." Wikipedia. Accessed May 17, 2017.* https://en.wikipedia.org/wiki/Naval_Air_Facility_Atsugi.

*"Niihau incident." Wikipedia. Accessed January 25, 2017.* https://en.wikipedia.org/wiki/Niihau_incident.

*"Nobusuke Kishi." Wikipedia. Accessed January 4, 2017.* https://en.wikipedia.org/wiki/Nobusuke_Kishi.

*"Occupation of Japan." Wikipedia. Accessed January 4, 2017.*
*https://en.wikipedia.org/wiki/Occupation_of_Japan.*

*Ohkubo, Masayuki. Interviewed by the author. November 26, 2016.*

*Oi, Mariko. "The man who saved Kyoto from the atomic bomb." BBC*
*News. August 09, 2015. Accessed January 18, 2017.*
*http://www.bbc.com/news/world-asia-33755182.*

*"Okayama University." WikiVisually. Accessed July 6, 2017.*
*http://wikivisually.com/wiki/Okayama_University.*

*OPERATION KETSU-GO. Accessed January 26, 2017.*
*https://fas.org/irp/eprint/arens/chap4.htm.*

*"Orphans tell of World War II internment ." CNN. Accessed May 17,*
*2017. http://www.cnn.com/US/9703/24/interned.orphans/.*

*"Pacific War." Wikipedia. September 28, 2017. Accessed December 6,*
*2016. https://en.wikipedia.org/wiki/Pacific_War.*

*"Pearl Harbor advance-knowledge conspiracy theory." Wikipedia.*
*Accessed December 6, 2016.*
*https://en.wikipedia.org/wiki/Pearl_Harbor_advance-*
*knowledge_conspiracy_theory.*

*"Pearl Harbor: The Truth." History. December 4, 2016.*

*Perloff, James. "Pearl Harbor: Scapegoating Kimmel and Short." The*
*New American. Accessed December 7, 2016.*
*http://www.thenewamerican.com/culture/history/item/4742-pearl-*
*harbor-scapegoating-kimmel-and-short.*

*Pletcher, Kenneth. "Bushidō." Encyclopædia Britannica. Accessed*
*December 14, 2016. https://www.britannica.com/topic/Bushido.*

*"Poston War Relocation Center." Wikipedia. Accessed March 28, 2017.*
*https://en.wikipedia.org/wiki/Poston_War_Relocation_Center.*

"POSTON". *Japanese American Veterans Association.* Accessed March 28, 2017. http://www.javadc.org/poston.htm.

"Rape during the occupation of Japan." *Wikipedia.* Accessed January 5, 2017. https://en.wikipedia.org/wiki/Rape_during_the_occupation_of_Japan.

"Recreation and Amusement Association." *Wikipedia.* Accessed January 5, 2017. https://en.wikipedia.org/wiki/Recreation_and_Amusement_Association.

"Religions - Shinto: Shinto and nationalism." *BBC.* September 17, 2009. Accessed January 17, 2017. http://www.bbc.co.uk/religion/religions/shinto/history/nationalism_1.sht ml.

"Renunciation Act of 1944." *Wikipedia.* Accessed January 31, 2017. https://en.wikipedia.org/wiki/Renunciation_Act_of_1944.

"Research Starters: Worldwide Deaths in World War II." *The National WWII Museum | New Orleans.* Accessed December 8, 2016. http://www.nationalww2museum.org/learn/education/for-students/ww2-history/ww2-by-the-numbers/world-wide-deaths.html.

"Ryoichi Sasakawa." *Wikipedia.* Accessed January 4, 2017. https://en.wikipedia.org/wiki/Ryoichi_Sasakawa.

Saiki, Patsy Sumie. *Ganbare!: an example of Japanese spirit.* Honolulu, HI: Mutual Pub., 2004.

Sakamoto, Hiroto. *E-mail interview by author.* July 4, ,2017.

"Senninbari." *Wikipedia.* Accessed January 4, 2017. https://en.wikipedia.org/wiki/Senninbari.

"Shibuya incident." *Wikipedia.* Accessed January 5, 2017. https://en.wikipedia.org/wiki/Shibuya_incident.

Shinmoto, Dorothy. *Interviewed by author.* March 25, ,2017.
218

"Shinto." Wikipedia. Accessed January 17, 2017.
https://en.wikipedia.org/wiki/Shinto.

"Surrender of Japan." Wikipedia. Accessed December 14, 2016.
https://en.wikipedia.org/wiki/Surrender_of_Japan.

Takahashi, Fusako. E-mail interview by author. April 14, 2017.

"Talk: Evacuation of Karafuto and Kuriles." Wikipedia. Accessed
August 15, 2017.
https://en.wikipedia.org/wiki/Talk:Evacuation_of_Karafuto_and_Kuriles.

"The Battle for Iwo Jima." The National WWII Museum | New
Orleans. Accessed December 8, 2016.
http://www.nationalww2museum.org/focus-on/iwo-jima-fact-sheet.pdf.

"The coup against the Emperor's broadcast that never was." The Japan
Times. Accessed December 22, 2016.
http://www.japantimes.co.jp/news/2015/08/06/national/history/coup-
emperors-broadcast-never/#.WFxQDX3yQkQ.

The Doolittle Raid, 1942. Accessed December 12, 2016.
http://www.eyewitnesstohistory.com/doolittle.htm.

"The Niihau Incident." HistoryNet. Accessed January 25, 2017.
http://www.historynet.com/the-niihau-incident.htm.

"Unit 731." Wikipedia. Accessed August 14, 2017.
https://en.wikipedia.org/wiki/Unit_731.

"US Initial Post-Surrender Policy for Japan." Wikipedia. Accessed
January 4, 2017. https://en.wikipedia.org/wiki/US_Initial_Post-
Surrender_Policy_for_Japan.

"Wayne M. Collins." Wikipedia. Accessed January 31, 2017.
https://en.wikipedia.org/wiki/Wayne_M._Collins.

William, Sydney Australia. "Skwirk Interactive Schooling." , The spread of communism after the Second World War, Australia in the Vietnam War Era, History Year 9, NSW | Online Education Home Schooling Skwirk Australia. Accessed December 12, 2016. http://www.skwirk.com/p-c_s-14_u-116_t-311_c-1051/communism-after-1945-background/nsw/communism-after-1945-background/australia-in-the-vietnam-war-era/the-spread-of-communism-after-the-second-world-war.

"World War II casualties." Wikipedia. Accessed December 6, 2016. https://en.wikipedia.org/wiki/World_War_II_casualties.

"World War II in the Pacific Japanese Unit 731Biological Warfare Unit." Unit 731. Accessed August 14, 2017. http://www.ww2pacific.com/unit731.html.

"WWII Japanese War Brides The Untold Story." Veterans Resources. Accessed January 6, 2017. http://www.veteransresources.org/wp-content/uploads/2016/10/Mil-Hist-WWII-Japanese-War-Brides.pdf.

Yasui, Holly. "Minoru Yasui Day in Denver." The Huffington Post. September 11, 2015. Accessed May 17, 2017. http://www.huffingtonpost.com/holly-yasui/minoru-yasui-day-in-denve_b_8123624.html.

Yoshida, Reiji. "Japan profited as opium dealer in wartime China." The Japan Times. Accessed March 29, 2017. http://www.japantimes.co.jp/news/2007/08/30/national/japan-profited-as-opium-dealer-in-wartime-china/#.WNQEJ33ySUk.

Yoshida, Reiji. "Opium King's ties believed went to the top." The Japan Times. Accessed March 29, 2017. http://www.japantimes.co.jp/news/2007/08/30/national/opium-kings-ties-believed-went-to-the-top/#.WNQDwX3ySUk.

"Yoshio Kodama." Wikipedia. Accessed January 4, 2017. https://en.wikipedia.org/wiki/Yoshio_Kodama.

*"Yumiko-chan incident."* Wikipedia. Accessed January 24, 2017. https://en.wikipedia.org/wiki/Yumiko-chan_incident.

*"Zaibatsu."* Wikipedia. September 24, 2017. Accessed January 4, 2017. https://en.wikipedia.org/wiki/Zaibatsu.

Made in the USA
Columbia, SC
07 February 2018